RAISING BOYS TO BE GOOD MEN

RAISING BOYS TO BE GOOD MEN

A Parent's Guide to Bringing Up
Happy Sons in a World Filled with
Toxic Masculinity

AARON GOUVEIA

Skyhorse Publishing

Skyhorse Publishing books may be purchased in bulk at special discounts for sales promotion, corporate gifts, fund-raising, or educational purposes. Special editions can also be created to specifications. For details, contact the Special Sales Department, Skyhorse Publishing, 307 West 36th Street, 11th Floor, New York, NY 10018 or info@skyhorsepublishing.com.

Skyhorse® and Skyhorse Publishing® are registered trademarks of Skyhorse Publishing, Inc.®, a Delaware corporation.

Visit our website at www.skyhorsepublishing.com.

10 9 8 7 6 5 4 3 2 1

Library of Congress Cataloging-in-Publication Data is available on file.
Library of Congress Control Number: 2020932654

Cover design by Erin Seaward-Hiatt
Cover photo credit: iStockphoto

Print ISBN: 978-1-5107-4941-2
Ebook ISBN: 978-1-5107-4942-9

Printed in the United States of America

Dedicated to MJ, Will, Sam, and Tommy.
I'm a better father, husband, and person because of you.
I love you with all my heart.

To my mom, who was always the voice of compassion
and kindness—even when I didn't want to hear it.

To my dad, who is my best friend and
everything a great dad should be.

Table of Contents

RAISING BOYS TO BE GOOD MEN

Introduction

When You're Part of the Problem

WHEN I BECAME A FATHER IN 2008, I HAD NEVER ENCOUN-tered the term *toxic masculinity.* Although Google searches for the term increased after the 2017 social movement of #MeToo when women in Hollywood reported Harvey Weinstein's crimes, and public exposure to the phrase spiked to peak levels when Gillette released its now infamous commercial in January 2019 criticizing toxic masculinity, I first heard about it in 2011. I had just accepted a part-time editor position with the Good Men Project and was spending countless hours reading essays by feminist authors. I rolled my eyes initially and silently lamented the "pussification of America," bristling at the thought that my strong, manly son would be feminized to the point of demoni-zation. Which is ironic, since, you know, that reaction was an example of classic toxic masculinity.

But when I stopped and listened to the people in my life, who are far more intelligent and thoughtful than I am, I realized something fairly disconcerting—not only is toxic masculinity real, I was living it out on a daily basis and running the risk of passing that mindset on to my three sons.

That's why, when my publisher suggested I write a book on raising boys in the age of toxic masculinity, the first thing out of my mouth was, "I think you've got the wrong guy." I guarantee that if you tell anyone who knew me in college that I would be writing this book many years later, they'd laugh. Then they'd get really confused and angry, because I had been representative of the problem for years (and still am, at times).

Back in 2008, I remember getting upset when my wife put pink socks on my infant son because I was worried it might make other people think he was "gay" or "effeminate." I didn't want any of my boys to be baptized, at least in part because I didn't like the idea of them in a christening dress (and also because of the Catholic Church's rampant child abuse and decades of cover-ups; but that's a different book). I would only shop in the blue-colored boy toy aisle, I scolded my oldest for throwing a baseball "like a girl," and I frequently used the phrase "man up" in a way that was unfortunately devoid of irony.

All to say that writing a book about a problem I had clearly contributed to for a long time felt like an instant no-go and massively hypocritical.

But the flip side of that argument is: who better to reach people potentially open to change than a convert? Just like I wouldn't want to read a book about getting sober from an author who has never had a drink in their lives, maybe all my (many, many, *many*) past mistakes might be recognized by readers who are in the same boat. The hope is that my experience will resonate and help readers take stock of the situation so we can start to build critical mass and fix this problem.

And yes, make no mistake, what's happening with boys and men today is a problem. A massive one that's silently and insidiously at the heart of so many societal ills. When I first shared the title of this book, *Raising Boys to Be Good Men*, a few transgender people in my circle of friends correctly pointed out that not all kids who are born male grow up to become men. I understand the criticism. But, the other side of the story is that my goal of writing this book isn't just to teach boys to grow up to be good people; it's about bringing them up in an environment of toxic masculinity where they must learn to survive a culture that makes dangerous assumptions and saddles them with superfluous baggage based solely on their genitals. In that way, I hope my transgender friends and I are in agreement, and I hope this book will capture the nuance that the book title can't.

Ever look at the totality of mass shootings and pinpoint the common denominator? Virtually all men. In an FBI list of active shooter incidents in the United States from 2000 to 2017, 241 out of 250 incidents identified involved male shooters. A majority of them white, many of them suffering from untreated or undertreated mental illness, and most of them just angry at women. In fact, while analyzing mass shootings from 2009 to 2018, the nonprofit Everytown for Gun Safety found that 54 percent of perpetrators had shot a current or former intimate partner or family member.[1] These are angry men with no coping mechanisms other than violence to express that rage.

The #MeToo movement? Men are overwhelmingly the perpetrators, using their systemic privilege and power as license to manipulate, harass, and abuse women to serve their own ends.

---

1 "Ten Years of Mass Shootings in the United States", *EveryTown for Gun Safety*, November 21, 2019, https://everytownresearch.org/massshootingsreports/mass-shootings-in-america-2009-2019/

These men do so without even thinking about it because it has always been the practiced "norm," safeguarded by other men in power in almost every industry.

The onslaught of heartbeat bills to weaken and even destroy Roe v. Wade? Legislation is perpetrated by mostly male legislators to criminalize the perfectly safe and legal medical procedure of abortion and strip women of bodily autonomy, usually without even knowing how the biological anatomy they're restricting works.

The gender wage gap? (A 2019 PayScale study finds women making 79 cents to every dollar that a similarly qualified man makes.[2]) Boys falling behind girls academically? Boys and men not seeking mental health treatment because of the idiotic notion that talking about your feelings is something only women do? According to the American Foundation for Suicide Prevention, men are committing suicide at a rate 3.54 times higher than women. All these problems and more—it's all part and parcel of toxic masculinity, and it all has to stop because it is crippling our boys.

I learned this firsthand one day in October 2018 when my middle son, Sam, then a five-year-old who had just started kindergarten, came home from school in shambles. He had been teased and bullied by the children in his class because he had had the audacity to wear red nail polish to school. Despite having done this in preschool for eighteen months prior to that day, with zero problems at all, once kindergarten hit, Sam was now dealing with a larger pool of kids from all kinds of backgrounds who were clearly already well-versed in traditional gender roles and they did *not* take kindly to a boy stepping into the realm of

---

2 "The State of the Gender Pay Gap 2019", *PayScale*, April 26, 2019, https://www.payscale.com/data/gender-pay-gap

"feminine" nail polish. He was told that nail polish is only for girls, to take it off immediately, and to never wear it again—because "boys don't do that." Up to that point, Sam had had no shame about painting his fingernails as it was something he had always done with his grandmother, my mom, a former manicurist. But after just one day of teasing and ridicule, he was ready to abandon it for fear of being seen as a girl.

I defended Sam via a Twitter thread that described what happened and talked about his innocence and the gender-neutral outlook he'd had all of his short life. My tweets included:

Sam is my middle child & he's a terror. A "boy's boy" as so many (not me) would say. He's rough and tumble, he's loud, he's always dirty, loves trucks, plays sports and knee drops me from the couch. But he also loves a lot of "girl" things.

So he proudly wore his red nail polish to kindergarten this morning because Sam has absolutely no concept of nail polish only being for girls or reason to think anyone would possibly have a problem with beautiful nails.

But his classmates did have a problem. A big one. Sam was ridiculed for being a boy with nail polish. They called him names and told him to take it off. This lasted the entire day.

When my wife picked him up from school he collapsed into her arms and cried uncontrollably. He was devastated at how other kids turned on him, even his friends. He asked them to stop but that just made it worse. Only 1 kid stood up for him.

My son is far from perfect but he's got a huge heart and empathy for miles. He finds beauty in everything around him and for 5 years he's never been afraid to be different because different has never meant 'bad.' Until now.

I know these kids are only in kindergarten but this toxic masculinity bullshit is LEARNED. Learned most of the time from parents. So parents, I hope you're proud. I hope this is what you wanted. I hope you're satisfied.

My wife and I spent five years successfully preaching tolerance, acceptance, and the importance of expression and your kids unraveled that in one school day. He now feels the shame you desperately want to associate with being different.

But I want you to know I talked to Sam and I told him those other kids are just jealous of his nails. I told him to wear an even brighter shade tomorrow. And I told him to ask these kids why they're so upset and see what they say.

I bet they don't know. I bet their parents don't even know. But what I do know is Sam is a goddamn fireworks show of a human being and I won't let that be dulled for a second by this restrictive bullshit that's been choking boys forever.

I told Sam he could take off the nail polish if he wanted but lots of guys wear it like Thor (@chrishemsworth) & Capt. Jack Sparrow. He asked if his fav football player @robgronkowski did. I'm not sure but I told him yes. Sorry, Gronk. But more importantly I told him it doesn't matter what anyone else does because what you wear and how you look should make YOU look good. And to hell with everyone else.

After careful consideration, he's leaving it on. Because he likes it and it makes him feel good. Then Sam's 10-year-old brother painted HIS nails in solidarity with his sibling, at which point I nearly cried.

Intolerant parents and their offspring scored a minor victory today but they won't win the war. I know that because the Sams of the world aren't going to suffer this bullshit anymore. Of that I have no doubt.

The thread went *super* viral to the tune of more than 80,000 likes, which led me and my family to appearances on the *TODAY Show*[3] and to be featured in positive articles in *Good Morning America*[4], *Mashable*[5], *People*[6], and international newspapers like *The Guardian*[7]. But it certainly wasn't all praise. People from all over the country also responded to tell me how terrible it is for a father to encourage a boy to paint his nails, labeling me a "beta male" and calling both Sam and me "gay." A particular low point was landing on the front page of *The Daily Stormer*,[8] an actual Neo-Nazi website, which tore into our physical features and denigrated me as a "beta cuck" who was ruining my son

---

3   Alex Fiquette, "5-year-old Who Was Bullied for Nail Polish Speaks Out," *TODAY Show*, January 28, 2019, https://www.today.com/video/5-year-old-who-was-bullied-for-nail-polish-speaks-out-1433049667793

4   Genevieve Shaw Brown, "Little Boy Bullied for Nail Polish Gets Confidence From Community of Strangers," *Good Morning America*, October 24, 2018, https://www.goodmorningamerica.com/family/story/boy-bullied-nail-polish-confidence-community-strangers-58697856

5   Victoria Rodriguez, "Meet Aaron Gouveia, the Dad Who Defended Son's Nail Polish in Viral Twitter Thread," *Mashable*, October 27, 2018, https://mashable.com/article/boy-wears-nail-polish-to-school-twitter-thread/

6   Michelle Boudin, "Dad Paints His Nails After 5-Year-Old Son Is Bullied for Wearing Polish: I 'Have Your Back!'," *People*, October24, 2018, https://people.com/human-interest/sam-gouveia-nail-polish-school-boston/

7   Miranda Bryant, "Father's Post on Bullied Son's Pink Nail Polish Sparks Outpouring of Support," *The Guardian,* October 25, 2018, https://www.theguardian.com/technology/2018/oct/25/fathers-post-on-bullied-sons-pink-nail-polish-sparks-outpouring-of-support

8   Luis Castillo, "Sadistic Cuck Sends Wife's Son to Kindergarten With Pink Nails, He Gets Bullied; Cuck Brags on Twitter," *Daily Stormer*, October 26, 2018, https://dailystormer.name/sadistic-cuck-sends-wifes-son-to-kindergarten-with-pink-nails-he-gets-bullied-cuck-brags-on-twitter/

and masculinity in general. The scary part is, just a decade ago, I would've agreed with all the critics (well, except for the Nazis). I would've been horrified at the thought of my manly son wearing "girly" shit, and I would have done everything in my power to either hide it or convince him not to wear it. I had been ignorant and uninformed, and I couldn't see with unclouded judgment the deserved criticisms of our patriarchal culture.

I wish I could pinpoint a specific moment in time when it all clicked. It was because of my job with the Good Men Project, where I edited essay after essay of thoughts on this topic. It was joining online forums and Facebook groups and getting to know the men I had been thoughtlessly mocking to realize their words had merit. But mostly, it was watching my kids get older and take up interests that didn't align with traditional masculinity, and feeling that natural parental instinct to protect and defend the people who are most precious to you. If my kids had been star athletes and had fallen into the "normal" pathways for boys, would I be writing this book? I'd like to think so, but I'm just not sure. Unfortunately, it seems people don't truly get it until it becomes personal when it happens to them or someone they know. That's why I hope this book will have an impact—reading about a parent's angst after bullies come for their son over nail polish is something that really can change minds.

We have a ton of girl power movements today, and I'm ecstatic that young girls are empowered and encouraged to lean into traditionally male-dominated fields and to be whoever and whatever they want. But that leniency is not often extended to boys. Girls are encouraged to wear pants and play sports and join the military, but watch what happens when boys try ballet. Or paint their fingernails. Or have the audacity to play with a baby doll. Add to that the sickening machismo and faux tough-guy-ism boys see from President Donald J. Trump on a daily basis, and you're left with an uphill battle when it comes to taking on harmful stereotypes and gender norms.

That's why I'm writing to all the parents who still tell their young sons to "rub some dirt on it" and who scold them for crying. Or who excuse clearly problematic behaviors with the response, "boys will be boys." This book is one small attempt to reach the people still willing to listen to reason. It's not meant to preach or shame, and it's certainly not an orchestrated attack on masculinity itself. There's a mistaken belief that those who criticize toxic masculinity are criticizing *everything* masculine—this couldn't be further from the truth. Caring for and protecting one's family; hard work; strength—these are some positives in men that are worthy of celebration. However, we need to reframe the discussion about what makes a "real man." Because I guarantee you that real men cry, real men will know to seek help when they need it, and real men do stay home with their kids.

It's not only possible to raise boys who aren't emotionally stifled and shoved into boxes; it's vital if we want a generation of men who can express their emotions in a healthy way, respect women, and help nurse society back to a halfway healthy place. That's why we need to illustrate the problems and talk about the small ways in which we can work toward solutions.

I guarantee that if a stubborn idiot like me can recognize he was once part of the problem and admit he was wrong, and then took the steps to become better, anyone can. And I also guarantee that if we don't change the way we treat and raise our boys, things are only going to get worse. Our boys are too important for us to fail, and when boys go bad, we *all* lose.

Chapter 1

The Bullshit Starts Before the Birth

IT'S CUSTOMARY TO START ANY STORY AT THE BEGINNING, BUT this crap starts before birth.

As a father of three boys (ages twelve, six, and four), I'm a grizzled veteran of the parenting wars. But many people reading this book might just be starting on their journeys, and if so, congratulations! And also, condolences. Because you're about to deal with a metric ton of gendered bullshit—and it starts yesterday.

One of the very first questions you'll be asked upon announcing your impending parenthood is: "Is it a boy or a girl?" This is *very important* to a great many people who just must know whether a penis is present so they can immediately start boxing your unborn child in with gendered colors and baby clothes that say wildly inappropriate and asinine things, or so they can bestow upon you countless clichés that make little to no sense.

These folks are usually well-meaning enough, but I was not prepared for how forceful they would be about demanding to know the sex. And frankly, it pissed me off.

"Well, I need to know if I'm buying pink or blue clothes."
"I'm knitting a blanket, and I need to know the color."
"Is it going to be a football player or a ballerina?"
Colors don't have genders!
If the blanket keeps the kid warm, it doesn't matter!
Boys and girls can do both those things!

Again, I know they mean well, and your Great Aunt Muriel probably isn't purposely trying to reinforce harmful gender stereotypes. But what she probably doesn't know is that these seemingly harmless decisions, such as color coding your baby, will have long-lasting effects and negative consequences that will stifle the potential and self-expression of your child from day zero. If this is an important issue to you (and it should be), there are some things you can do to blunt the unintended harm this kind of antiquated thinking causes.

PARENTING TIP #1: Don't find out/tell anyone the sex of the baby

Granted, this is not for the faint of heart or the Type A personalities who thrive on planning and details. I get it. When we were expecting our oldest child in 2007, I was all in on finding out what we were having as soon as humanly possible, and I just figured that my wife, MJ, was in the same boat.

Nope.

At our eighteen-week ultrasound, the tech asked if we were ready to find out the sex. Before I could utter a word, my wife said, "No thanks, we want it to be a surprise." I couldn't believe what I was hearing—and I'm not proud to say that I was furious. As we argued right there in the exam room in front of the increasingly uncomfortable ultrasound technician, MJ calmly explained her reasoning. This was "the ultimate surprise" that could never be replicated. Plus, it would keep all the blue/pink nonsense at bay for a little while longer, and it'd be fun to have people guess.

But I wasn't buying it. At all. I asked her if I could find out on my own and not tell her, but she reminded me that I'm a terrible secret-keeper and that I'd spill the beans even if I didn't mean to. I asked if the tech could write it down on a piece of paper so we could open it if MJ changed her mind, but she didn't want to succumb to temptation. So that was nixed, as well.

Then, when she realized her arguments weren't landing, she pulled the trump card. "Well, I'm sorry you don't like it, but this baby is inside *me* and therefore it's *my* decision—and we're not finding out."

I stared at her and saw nothing but determination. I desperately looked at the ultrasound tech, who was doing her best to shrink into the corner of the room and disappear, and I ridiculously asked her if I had any recourse, legal or otherwise, to allow me to find out the sex. That's when she stared at me like I was a complete moron (warranted) and uttered the words, "Sorry, but she's right."

With steam coming from my ears, I left that office without knowing the sex. And you know what? It was a fantastic decision by my wife and one we'd end up repeating two more times.

Why did I have a change of heart? How did I ultimately come to admit that I was wrong?

First of all, it really was a surprise like no other. Being in the delivery room and watching the person you love bring another person you love into the world is already pretty damn magical, but hearing the doctor tell you that you're having a son or a daughter after more than nine months of anticipation? Unforgettable. Sure, it would've been a great reveal moment right there in the exam room at eighteen weeks, too, but waiting really did make it better for us.

More important, MJ was right about how not finding out the sex delays all the gendered bullshit we parents have to face for at least a little while. Plus, it pissed everyone off to no end, which was an added bonus for this born contrarian. With the sex not yet determined, it forced people to think outside the box a little bit. The blankets people made for us were green and yellow. The clothes they gifted us at MJ's baby shower were gender neutral. The decorations for the baby's room were animals fit for any child rather than strictly sports-themed or princess-oriented. Hey, I'm a huge sports fan, but if I had a son, I didn't want the pigeonholing to start even before my baby could play catch; and if I had a daughter, I refused to watch an entire bedroom be turned into a sea of Pepto Bismol pink before she could name her favorite color. Point being, the wonderful thing about babies is their limitless potential, so why place arbitrary caps on what they can be? It's difficult to remember that your kids are going to become their own people, and not mini versions of you, but stopping yourself from boxing them in from day one is a precious gift that will pay dividends in the long run.

However, there was one weird side effect of not telling people what we were having: it unleashed the old wives' tales. In the absence of a conclusive ultrasound, people were forced to resort to outrageous and hilarious myths they had heard from their grandparents and great-grandparents. You know, such as if you're carrying high then it's a girl, while boys hang low. Or if MJ was craving sweets, that meant it was a girl, but sour translated to boy (because I guess boys can't be sweet?!).

But at least that stuff was mildly amusing. Know what's not? The highly questionable gender-stereotypical comments that are all too often bestowed on your baby in jest, as if that meant they were okay: "If it's a boy, this town better lock up its daughters" or "If it's a girl, you better buy a gun." Excuse me? So if I'm having a boy, you're saying he's going to exit the womb hungry for not only his mother's breast but also every boob out there? That he'll be a rampaging sexual beast so unruly he won't be able to practice a modicum of self-control to the point that women will have to be locked away while in his sexually insatiable presence? And if it's a girl, I'll suddenly need a firearm? That now that I'm the father of a daughter, the first thing on my mind is securing an AR-15 and keeping it handy so I can scare the living shit out of some poor boy who dares to look my daughter's way or—gasp—asks her to go on a date?

I can already hear some of you thinking: *calm down, they're just jokes.* But no, they're not. Because automatically assuming that a little boy will become a man who will be a slave to his sexual desires is setting him up to fail, and arming yourself to gatekeep your little girl's virginity is creepy as hell. Not only are those things not funny, they're part of a harmful set of stereotypes that continue to insidiously promote the harmful misconception that it's OK, even acceptable, for boys to be oafish, sex-obsessed idiots, while girls are precious jewels that need to be protected from the presence of men. I imagine if you happen to be a parent of both a boy and a girl, you'll notice how ironic these two belief systems are when placed together.

Don't take the bait, and don't get off on the wrong track early. If you can, it's best to skip this portion of the nonsense altogether, which will force the people around you to think about and treat your future child a little differently—in a nongendered way that is not limited by an imagined boundary. It won't kill anyone (and it'll entertain you to no end watching them squirm), and it just might change their thinking ever so slightly.

PARENTING TIP #2: Avoid the gender reveal party

Maybe it's not everyone else who needs to know the sex of the baby. Maybe it's *you* who has to know—so you can engage in one of the most annoyingly narcissistic developments of this modern age: throwing a gender reveal party.

For the blessedly uninitiated, a gender reveal party is when a person or couple decides it's not enough to just tell their close friends and family. Instead, they need to do it via a surprise reveal that is caught on video and that lifts them to internet virality in 17 seconds of fleeting fame. People cut into cakes that are either blue or pink on the inside. They open boxes with balloons that are either blue or pink. They culturally appropriate piñatas to discover their baby's sex when—wait for it—blue or pink confetti pops out. Flares, smoke bombs, confetti poppers . . . you get the idea (although I wish no one ever had in the first place).

There was even that infamous gender reveal party in Arizona when a Border Patrol Agent found out the sex of his baby by shooting a package of colored explosive, which ignited nearby grasses and shrubs, causing the Sawmill Fire. Yup—a gender reveal party ended up scorching 47,000 acres of land to the tune of $8 million in damages after it took nearly eight hundred fire-fighters to put it out.[9] Consider for a moment how ridiculous it is to include an instrument of death in a ceremony meant to honor the impending arrival of new life. It was a boy, by the way. A boy who (fingers crossed) will have other male role models to guide his way in addition to his gun-wielding, fire-starting father who just *had* to blow some shit up.

---

9   Andrea Diaz, "Officials Release Video From a Gender Reveal Party That Ignited a 47,000-Acre Wildfire," *CNN*, November 28, 2018, https://www.cnn.com/2018/11/27/us/arizona-gender-reveal-party-sawmill-wildfire-trnd/index.html

So, I'm not exaggerating when I tell you gender reveal parties are a legitimate threat to our planet.

But, seriously, one of my main issues with gender reveal parties is that these spectacles are predicated again on the blue-is-for-boys and pink-is-for-girls binary, which drives me nuts. Pink is not a strictly feminine color. In fact, the trade publication *Earnshaw's Infants' Department* published a June 1918 article that advised: "The generally accepted rule is pink for the boys, and blue for the girls. The reason is that pink, being a more decided and stronger color, is more suitable for the boy, while blue, which is more delicate and dainty, is prettier for the girl."[10] Now that's problematic in and of itself, but it just goes to show you that the idea of gendered colors is a cultural construct—and that boys can like pink very much. My middle son is living proof of that, and he's no less a boy because of it.

Another terribly sad side effect of many gender reveal parties is the sex isn't all that's revealed. Many soon-to-be parents hoping for one sex over the other end up having their disappointment caught on camera on a day that should be decidedly and monumentally positive.

Finally, these parties are wrongly labeled from the start. It can't be a "gender reveal," since parents have absolutely no idea what gender their kids will ultimately be (sex refers to the biological traits assigned at birth, while gender is an identity as expressed by an individual). All this party really does is assign kids labels before they've even entered the world and certainly prior to them having any opportunity to figure out their gender identity. The simple fact of the matter is your unborn child, who let's say is born biologically male, may not identify with their assigned sex.

---

10 Jeanne Maglaty, "When Did Girls Start Wearing Pink," *Smithsonian.com*, April 7, 2011, https://www.smithsonianmag.com/arts-culture/when-did-girls-start-wearing-pink-1370097/

All this to say, what's wrong with just celebrating life instead of unnecessarily restricting kids to a gender identity that might not even stick?

If you still don't believe me, take it from Jenna Karvunidis herself—the mom blogger who literally invented the gender reveal party in 2008.[11] In a July 2019 post on Facebook, Karvunidis expressed regret at having inadvertently started a fad she now believes to be negative due to gender stereotyping. She writes: "Who cares what gender the baby is? I did at the time because we didn't live in 2019 and didn't know what we know now— that assigning focus on gender at birth leaves out so much of their potential and talents that have nothing to do with what's between their legs." Oh, and the plot twist? The daughter whose sex was revealed in that very first gender reveal party is now an eleven-year-old who regularly wears suits. Because: kickass, gender-bending irony.

My advice? Be thrilled you're having a healthy baby, and rest assured that your excitement will not be dulled one iota whether it's a boy or a girl. Just tell people you're expecting and celebrate new life rather than focusing on sex.

And stop shooting shit. Seriously.

PARENTING TIP #3: Dads–go to baby classes and get in the delivery room

When MJ was pregnant, everyone said there was no single instruction manual for raising kids. That was good news to me, because

---

11 Tanya Chen, "The Mom Blogger Who Had the First Viral Gender Reveal Has a New Perspective After Raising Her Daughter," *Buzzfeed*, July 26, 2019, https://www.buzzfeednews.com/article/tanyachen/mom-who-invented-the-gender-reveal-cake-changed-her-mind

even if an instruction manual did exist, I wouldn't have read it. Because real men don't need to be told how to do anything, amirite?! (I swear, writing this book caused me massive pain whenever I looked back and reflected on just how stupid I was.)

While it's true that there's no definitive instruction manual because every child and parent is on a different journey, there are some universal truths and best practices that every parent should prepare themselves for before the birth. The good news is these can come in the form of childbirth classes, which are available at most hospitals or family planning centers at little to no cost to you. You'll learn about the process of checking in to the hospital, you'll get to tour the birthing room, you'll practice changing diapers on a doll, and you'll learn about different kinds of baby products. You'll also probably watch a video of a real woman giving birth.

That last one is what got me.

Look, I know basic biology, so I understand where babies come from and how they're delivered. But I knew that information on a theoretical level. I knew it from movies where a beautiful woman screams in pain for thirteen seconds, grunts once, and delivers a perfectly clean, Abercrombie-model-type, six-month-old baby, all while somehow keeping her makeup perfectly intact. But the video I watched in childbirth class abruptly and violently cured me of any delusions of Hollywood grandeur.

You see everything. The labor, the painful pushing, the baby crowning, a small human being the size of a watermelon somehow coming out of a miraculously expanding opening the size of a lemon, and finally the end result—a tiny, wrinkled, scrunchy-faced alien that looks nothing like the gleamingly clean cinematic babies in every rom-com. You also see the "other stuff." Oh yeah, there's other stuff. The afterbirth was the toughest for me, personally. They wheeled a trash barrel in the room for easy disposal. A *trash barrel*! We live in an age of unparalleled technological wonders, so I had imagined there would be some fancy way to deal with this stuff (perhaps a Roomba for placentas), but no. A trash barrel. And the mother in the video damn near filled it, too.

I looked around at the other men in the class, and it was clear we were going to leave that room vastly different men than when we had entered. One guy muttered, "No way, I ain't here for all that," and for a split second, I nodded in agreement. But then, in a rare moment of clarity, I caught myself.

Of course I was going to be in that room, because the woman I had married would be delivering the baby I had helped make. If my first official act as a father was to disappear at the first sight that made me uncomfortable, then what-the-hell kind of tone would that set? Plus, what about the woman writhing in pain on the delivery bed? Men need to realize she doesn't get to leave, either!

Also, childbirth is beautiful. (Well, not the placenta, at least visually.) When taken in its totality, the experience of bringing new life into the world was one of the most thrilling, mind-bending, ridiculously meaningful things I've ever experienced. Some guys will tell you (in all seriousness) that they don't want to witness the birth because they'll never fondly look at a vagina ever again, but that's not just ridiculous—it's toxic. If anything, it gave me a whole new respect for vaginas, and I love my wife a billion times more for being a strong, brave, kickass woman who delivered three mammoth-sized boys.

So, dads: take the childbirth classes and be in the room so you can start out life as a new dad by being present. Taking these classes is a sign that you care enough about the new adventure you're embarking on together. Showing up for your partner is half the damn battle of fatherhood, and you'll demonstrate that she's not in this alone and that she can count on you to be there for her and your children now and in the future. Don't let toxic masculinity and male fragility rob you of an indescribable moment you will never be able to replicate. Remember: real men show up.

And moms: don't let men off the hook. Having soon-to-be dads involved in the process is not some Herculean ask or unreasonable expectation. Treat it for what it is—the bare minimum of what a decent partner should be doing. If you start doling out gold stars to men simply for doing what should already be expected of them, the bar will be set low and no one would be surprised when men only rise high enough to barely scrape it. Also, a good thing to keep in mind is the hesitancy some men express isn't always due to laziness—it can be fear, anxiety, depression, or a host of other reasons. If your male partner won't talk to you, suggest a friend, local dads' group, or doctor.

PARENTING TIP #4: It's OK to talk about miscarriage

Welcome to the unhappiest section of this book. I wish I didn't have so much experience with this particular subject, but despite having three children, my wife was pregnant a total of eight times. We had three successful births, four miscarriages in the first and second trimester, and one medically necessary abortion due to Sirenomelia (aka Mermaid Syndrome) that nearly broke us as a couple (more on this later in the book).

While this is not a topic that most people are comfortable talking about, it's still a necessary one: statistics show that between 10 and 20 percent of all pregnancies end in a miscarriage.[12] Despite

---

12 "Miscarriage," Mayo Clinic, accessed September 15, 2019, https://www.chicagomanualofstyle.org/tools_citationguide/citation-guide-1.html#cg-website

the prevalence of miscarriage, it's still a subject only discussed in hushed tones, and mostly by women, which is too bad because the emotional fallout is felt by everyone.

I was twenty-seven years old when MJ told me I was going to be a dad—and I was so damn excited. She took me out to dinner and tossed a paper bag my way that contained what I thought to be a thermometer (except this thermometer said "Pregnant" on it) and the world's smallest Boston Red Sox outfit. I tried to hold back the tears, but the dam burst almost immediately, and within seconds I was overcome with emotion and bawling my eyes out. After dropping to my knees in the middle of the restaurant and kissing her belly, I tearfully—and, now that I think about it, probably scarily for the other diners—screamed to anyone who would listen that I was going to be a father.

Just like that, our family plans fell into place in my head. We started talking about names, whether it'd be a boy or a girl, where we needed to move to for good school systems—and we also hoped the baby would look like MJ instead of me. I thought about youth sports and fishing trips and Father's Day—right down to my kid being named valedictorian at Harvard and thanking me in his or her graduation speech. It was overwhelming, but in the most wonderful way because, at that moment, literally anything was possible. The unlimited potential was exciting beyond words.

I'll never forget the moment that happened two weeks later. I remember MJ's panicked screams from the bathroom, where I rushed to, and not knowing precisely what was in the toilet but inherently understanding that this was bad. I recall the fear of the unknown and the distinct feeling of helplessness that envelops you when the person you love most is completely distraught—and there isn't a goddamn thing you can do to fix it. Which brought me to my next question: what should *I* do?

Most men are taught to be strong, silent, and stoic in the face of all danger and adversity. Luckily, my father is the communicator in my parents' relationship, and I grew up with a wonderful model for open and honest communication. I know he would've wanted me to upfront with her about how I was feeling. But in that moment, I panicked and flicked on the switch deep in my subconscious and harnessed my prehistoric caveman DNA: I went into "protector" mode and immediately went about trying to fix one problem at a time to soothe my wife. We had to get to the doctor, find out what was going on, make sure she was OK, and then figure out a path forward to try again. I must've asked my wife how she was doing roughly ten thousand times that week. Our family and friends were spectacular and surrounded her with kindness and warmth, and many of the women in our lives conveyed their own miscarriage stories, of which they had never previously spoken. It was cathartic in a way, a sort of melancholic beauty that I couldn't help but admire. And, if we're being honest, one that I was jealous of.

Men dealing with miscarriage often find themselves in a completely unnatural, unnerving, and unsure predicament. Mainly, we don't know what our role is supposed to be or how we're supposed to act. I had assumed that it was my job to stay strong for my wife; I had assumed that I didn't have the right to get all weepy myself. After all, it was her body, and she was dealing with the physical repercussions. How could I feel pity for myself when she was hurting so much? Also, what form was my sadness even supposed to take? Did I really lose a baby? Should I mourn this baby? For that matter, should I even consider this a baby? As a man, could I allow myself to cry over a nonviable collection of cells that didn't have a form? Or a name? I've known parents who have lost living, breathing children, and I couldn't for the life of me consider where my own grief stood with theirs. I also distinctly remember that no one asked me how *I* was doing during that time. If they weren't asking, I took that to mean that there was no reason for them to ask. So, I bottled up my own emotions and transformed them into what I thought MJ needed—a rock. A hard thing for her to lean on amid the waves. An unfeeling, inanimate object.

Of course, it was a really stupid idea that backfired tremendously.

It turned out I was deeply mourning the loss of potential, and all of that resentment and disappointment festered and boiled up inside of me. I thought no one would notice, but my wife sure did, and it strained our marriage quite a bit. It wasn't until she threw down the gauntlet and forced me to make an appointment with a counselor that I realized how traumatic the whole thing had been for me. Once I got over the guilt of admitting that my trauma was real, I ventured online and sought out groups dealing with fatherhood, pregnancy, and pregnancy loss. And that's when something miraculous happened.

I found my people online. Maybe it's the anonymity of the internet, but I was able to be honest with people in these groups in a way that I hadn't been able to before. Soon the floodgates opened, and I was talking to men everywhere who were going through the same struggle and feeling the same uncertainty and guilt. Here we were, men from all over the world, living in the most interconnected era humanity has ever seen, and yet we were all stuck in our little man boxes, cowed by toxic masculinity and the fear of being seen as weak. But you know what? Admitting your fears so you can deal with them and seeking help when you need it isn't weak—it's the epitome of strength.

Miscarriage is hard on everyone, but it's not just a woman's issue. As I'm sure most women who have been through this will attest, they don't want an unfeeling automaton who bottles up all his feelings. They want a true partner who commiserates with the sense of loss and disappointment and isn't afraid to show how much he cares. Too few men realize they can still be pillars of strength *and* emotionally intelligent people at the same time, despite what the bullies or faux macho idiots say. Toxic masculinity robs men of being good partners and of being true to themselves, so men need to start parenthood off on the right foot by building a solid foundation of emotional availability.

PARENTING TIP #5: Don't assume you're immune to toxic masculinity

In my not-so-scientific findings based on meandering around the internet, talking with thousands of dads, and even joining father groups and speaking at parenting conferences, I believe people are split into a few groups when it comes to the topic of toxic masculinity.

First of all, you have the people who don't even recognize the term and who couldn't tell you what the patriarchy is, yet they unknowingly live it every single day. This is their normal; it's their natural state. And if they're not open to learning about what they don't know, they probably aren't going to change.

Next, you've got those who feel discomforted by toxic masculinity even if they don't know it has a name. They silently believe something is wrong with how most of the men in their lives behave; however, they still resort to the default because it's all they know, especially if they were raised or currently live in more conservative areas. The good news with these folks is that there's hope, and sometimes all it takes is a conversation or reading a few articles (or books like this one) that describe the problem for it to click. These people can be empowered, and they have the potential to break the cycle and raise emotionally intelligent boys who are more readily equipped to battle toxic masculinity as they mature.

Then you have the people who *should* know better but who still fall into the trap and revert to toxic masculinity without realizing it, simply because they already believe themselves to be "woke" and, therefore, immune to toxic thoughts and behaviors.

I'm not proud to admit that I belong to this latter category, and for a while, I didn't even believe I was a member. After all, I had grown up with a feminist mother and an ultra-liberal dad who still says "I love you" and gives me a kiss every time I see him. I went to a liberal arts college and read Erica Jong and took a Virginia Woolf class. I run in feminist online circles, I vow to smash the patriarchy, I voted for Hillary Clinton, and I rose to fleeting global internet fame in 2018 when I stood up for my five-year-old son who was being bullied for wearing nail polish to kindergarten.

But sometimes, especially whenever my masculinity feels threatened, I'll slip back into old habits without even realizing it. Maybe I called the quarterback of whichever team my beloved New England Patriots were playing that week "a little bitch." Perhaps I dismissed a female political candidate not because she wasn't qualified, but because 2016 scared me and I thought she didn't have enough "likability." Or maybe I felt a shockingly unexpected but massive flood of relief when I got a job that paid more than my wife, who had been the breadwinner for years. Actually, there's no *maybe* involved—all of those things happened to me despite my education and progressive upbringing. I thought that because I knew about the dangers of the patriarchy and toxic masculinity, I was automatically immune to them, and this is very dangerous—probably even more dangerous than the people who have never been exposed to these ideas.

All this to say: if you truly want to fix the problem and be part of the solution, never stop questioning and examining what you're thinking or how you're acting. Actively combating toxic masculinity is a daily practice, not a single one-time event that happened in your past. And if you can do it now, before your baby is born, then you'll be better prepared to become a fitting role model.

It's extraordinarily difficult to recognize that you might be part of the problem, especially if you fancy yourself a progressive, but self-reflection and a willingness to work on yourself is a crucial component of finding a solution to this mess. So, as you prepare to become a parent, get it in your head that there's no finish line when it comes to ridding ourselves of toxic masculinity. It's too socially embedded and ingrained in all of us—men and women—for you to believe you're impervious to it. So, just be mindful that it takes a lifetime of work to make a difference.

It's worth it.

Chapter 2

Congratulations, You're a Parent— Welcome to the Jungle

T HE BIRTH OF A CHILD IS A GLORIOUS, WONDERFUL THING. Holding your baby for the first time, hearing them laugh, feeling them grab your finger while they look at you, and somehow just knowing that *they* know you'll be there for them always and forever? It's downright magical. Even changing diapers is a novelty you don't mind (at first).

But, on the flip side, it does not take very long for parenthood to test you when it throws some problematic shit your way in a hurry and forces you to question some of your own gender misconceptions.

The crazy part is that most of it seems benign on the surface, and a ton of it is unspoken. For instance, did you ever think about who is going to cook the meals? Who knows what to do if the baby is running a fever? Who is responsible for coordinating doctor appointments and remembering to bring along that little blue baby book with all your baby's statistics? For that matter, who is going to research vaccinations (and please, for the love of all things holy, *vaccinate your kids*)?

In a lot of traditional, heterosexual relationships, it's simply assumed that women will take care of these things while men bring home the proverbial bacon. I know that's what *I* thought. In fact, my wife was the primary breadwinner of the family who worked a ton of hours, which meant I would be the one doing those things once my oldest was born. It just goes to show how insidious gender stereotypes are, and how they had managed to burrow into my head. Additionally, when I was a kid, my mom took care of the block and tackle components of parenting, and that was all I knew. All this to say, more couples need to talk about household and baby chores and splitting responsibilities at the outset, and men need to realize that part of these responsibilities are going to be on their plate.

Now, let's talk about some critical junctures that occur immediately after a baby is born.

PARENTING TIP #6: Take maternity/paternity leave (if you can)

Let's get one thing straight: the United States is ridiculously behind the curve when it comes to offering parents paid leave, which is nothing short of shameful. The International Leave Network conducted a study of forty developed nations in 2016[13] to examine their leave policies and found that the US was one of two countries that didn't offer some sort of mandatory paid leave

13 Alison Koslowski, Sonja Blum, Peter Moss, "12th International Review of Leave Policies and Related Research 2016," *International Leave Network*, June 2016, https://www.leavenetwork.org/fileadmin/user_upload/k_leavenetwork/annual_reviews/2016_Full_draft_20_July.pdf

for new fathers. Despite a policy brief from the US Department of Labor called "Why Parental Leave For Fathers Is So Important For Working Families"[14] that states that paternity leave (of several weeks or months) "can promote parent-child bonding, improve outcomes for children, and even increase gender equity at home and at the workplace," only 13 percent of men who took parental leave were paid. Although unpaid leave is available via the Family Medical Leave Act (FMLA), many families can't afford to have both parents (or sometimes even one) not receiving a paycheck. Already, not enough mothers get paid leave in this country.

But let's back up for a second, because the problem with paternity and maternity leave doesn't rest entirely with the government failing to offer it.

Since it is women's bodies that endure the trauma of childbirth, many men in heterosexual relationships (myself included) are focused on the recovery of their significant others and do not even consider taking time off for themselves. This is silly when you think about it, because what better way to help women recover than to be home doing chores and taking care of the baby so they don't have to do everything?

But more than that, there's a cultural stigma associated with paternity leave. Namely, if you take time off for the birth of a baby or at the time of an adoption, you're perceived as "soft" because "real men" are expected to work and provide. Furthermore, there exists the very real possibility that men who take paternity leave at work will be subject to discrimination via being passed over for promotions and raises.

In 2014, New York Mets infielder Daniel Murphy was publicly blasted for taking paternity leave instead of immediately

---

14 "DOL Policy Brief, Paternity Leave: Why Parental Leave for Fathers is So Important for Working Families," United States Department of Labor, 1-6.

going back to work. Murphy, who missed the first two games of the season for the birth of his son, was lambasted by sports radio hosts Boomer Esiason, Craig Carton, and Mike Francesa.[15] Esiason said he would've had his wife schedule a C-section before the start of the season, while his co-host Carton said, "You get your ass back to your team and you play baseball . . . there's nothing you can do, you're not breastfeeding the kid." Esiason's suggestion to have an elective C-section (which he later apologized for) was especially troubling. A C-section is a major surgery that significantly extends recovery time, meaning that dads should be home for even longer to help their wives recover. Call me crazy, but I don't think sidelining your wife for a couple of extra weeks just so you can go back to work sooner makes you a "real man." Real men take care of their families.

According to a 2013 report by the Boston College Center for Work & Family, "The New Dad: A Work (and Life) in Progress,"[16] only 1 in 20 fathers took more than two weeks off after the birth of a child, with a mere 1 in 100 taking more than four weeks. Despite 77 percent of dads in the study saying they want to spend more time with their family, the reality of working life and the demands of their jobs don't seem to allow it.

My experience with paternity leave runs the gamut. When my oldest was born in 2008, I was working as a reporter at a newspaper with no paid leave options, so I was forced to take one of my

---

15 Matt Murray, "Radio Host Rips MLB Player for Paternity Leave, Suggests C-Section Before Season," *TODAY Show*, April 3, 2014, https://www.today.com/parents/radio-host-rips-mlb-player-paternity-leave-suggests-c-section-2D79476676

16 Brad Harrington, Fred Van Deusen, Jennifer Sabatini Fraone, "The New Dad: A Work (and Life) In Progress," *Boston College Center for Work and Family*, 2013, https://www.bc.edu/content/dam/files/centers/cwf/research/publications/researchreports/The%20New%20Dad%202013_A%20Work%20and%20Life%20in%20Progress

two available weeks of vacation as a makeshift paternity leave. While I was happy to have that time, it leads me to my next tip.

PARENTING TIP #7: Dads—stagger your leave if possible

I didn't know any better with my first child, so I took my leave right after my son was born. Although this seems logical, it turned out to be less than ideal for a few reasons you couldn't possibly know unless you've gone through it.

First of all, you're spending at least a couple of days in the hospital following a vaginal birth, and up to four or five days if it's a C-section. If you only have a week of leave, that wipes out a bunch of time right there. And while no circumstances are ever the same, many couples have family around who will be ever-present immediately following the birth. If you can have someone stay and help out the week of the birth, I recommend banking your time and taking it in a couple of weeks after the birth once the help is gone and the parenting grind of no sleep and constant wake-ups truly starts to hit home.

Those few weeks following the birth was when my wife needed me the most, but by that time I had used up all my leave and we couldn't afford to take unpaid FMLA. When I had to go back to work, I was out of time and options, a confused and harried new dad bidding a teary-eyed farewell to a wife struggling to take care of herself and a new baby. The stress from not having enough time at home quickly began to impact my work, resulting in an unhappy and unproductive employee who felt like he was constantly drowning.

I'll always feel guilty about that because I think it could've been mitigated had I used my time a little more wisely.

PARENTING TIP #8: Dive fully and deeply into your leave and tell everyone you took it

When my next two kids were born, I was in a much better position. I had taken a job at IBM, where I was granted two fully paid weeks of leave in 2013 when my second son was born, and then six weeks of fully paid leave when we had our third in 2015. And let me tell you, I used every damn bit of it. Not just because I wanted to be there for my kids and my wife, but also because I wanted other men I worked with to know that there's nothing wrong with a man taking leave. The truth is, you can take leave without fear of corporate punishment, and ultimately being an involved dad with a better work-life balance makes you a better employee.

It's also not enough just to take it—you have to really put in the work. More than one person asked me how my vacation was when I came back from paternity leave, which bugged the shit out of me. Anyone who actively cares for a newborn in the weeks after they're born knows it's the furthest thing from a vacation. Especially if there are extenuating circumstances, such as post-partum depression, colic, or other health issues.

My paternity leave consisted of taking care of my wife. It also involved supervising my oldest son's transition from only child to big brother. I made sure that he had a lunch packed and that he was sent to school on time, while also ensuring the baby had everything he needed. Most important, I had the time to bond with my baby. I held him, changed him, got up at night to support my wife during feedings, learned his sounds, and developed a routine.

There are those who will claim that dads are just in the way because they can't breastfeed and that they lack the parenting DNA that moms have. Don't listen to any of that toxic BS that contributes to labor inequality at home. I went to breastfeeding classes with my wife so I could be a second set of ears for whenever she was at her wit's end when the baby wouldn't latch. I took an infant CPR course because I knew that I should know what to do in every potential emergency situation. Women are in no way biologically predisposed to parenthood, and there's no secret manual imprinted in their DNA that makes them better caregivers. Dads who won't or can't take the opportunity to dive into their leave will lose out on so much of the initial experience that serves as a foundation for fatherhood down the road, because paternity leave allows men to be active participants in parenting, as opposed to bystanders.

There's no greater satisfaction than taking the time to learn which of your baby's sounds means it's time for a diaper change versus when your baby needs something to eat. I won't lie, it's hard work. But it's worth it, and then some.

PARENTING TIP #9: Don't accept different standards for moms and dads

Whether you take parental leave or not, one thing is for certain—eventually, you're going to have to leave the house with the baby. We headed out to Walmart when our oldest son was just a week old to buy some diaper cream and other essentials, and I ended up receiving a whole lot of unexpected knowledge.

I entered the store with MJ, who was carrying Will in a sling. I distinctly remember walking in front of them, realizing that I was involuntarily thinking of myself as a bodyguard or even an offensive lineman, ready to clear the way for my wife and son and pummel anyone who came too close. As we made our way through the aisles and finally to the section with an outrageous number of butt cream products, we got a few looks from people, eyeing our baby and lavishing him with comments like "too cute" and "ooooooh, look at the little one!" Nothing unusual or unexpected. But then MJ said she wasn't feeling well and had to go to the bathroom, so I took Will out of the sling and cuddled him close to me while MJ took off.

That's when it started.

One by one, like mysterious clockwork, women of all ages began coming up to me to pay their compliments.

"Oh, what a good daddy holding you like that!"

"Isn't mommy lucky to have daddy here taking care of you!"

"Looks like it's daddy's turn to babysit today!"

Now, I want to be very honest, and I'll tell you that I saw absolutely nothing wrong with this at first. In fact, I was damn well reveling in it. Because why wouldn't I? There I was, a new dad being all dad-ly, with all these people telling me how wonderful I was. What's better than that? As someone who definitely likes being in the spotlight and who craves a bit of attention from time to time, I was loving life in all my new dad glory.

It wasn't until after the millionth person paid me a compliment and MJ scoffed loudly and rolled her eyes that I even knew anything was wrong at all. When I asked her what could possibly be the problem, the following conversation ensued.

"You're being praised just for holding Will," MJ said.

"No, they just like seeing an involved dad. Nothing wrong with that," I fired back.

MJ dropped the hammer. "Oh really? How many times have you seen random people come up to me to tell me I'm a great mom just because I'm holding Will in a department store?"

Shit.

She continued, "Meanwhile, you're Dad of the Year just because you're actually paying attention to your kid even though you're supposed to? That's crap! And honestly, how are you not upset when people say you're 'babysitting'? You're Will's dad, not a babysitter. You can't babysit your own kid!"

As usual, she was absolutely right, and I was stunned at my own blindness to something that should've been crystal clear. The bar is set so low for dads that we are thrown a parade just for doing the bare minimum, while women are expected to do those things without so much as a "good job."

I know it seems counterintuitive, and even rude, to push back when someone gives you (what they consider to be) a compliment. I understand it may seem odd when someone who speaks up for more public recognition of fathers tells you to ironically shun praises when they're showered upon you. But that's exactly what we need to do—both men and women—so that we can cultivate realistic and positive expectations for parents, and so that we don't foster overly gendered roles and unfair standards for moms versus dads.

So, how can parents do this without losing friends and alienating people who are probably just trying to be nice or friendly?

Just have some tact. Remember, these are people who are trying to compliment you but are unwittingly falling into a trap they may not even know is there. Don't snap at them, but push back gently and aim to educate instead of scold. For instance, if you're a dad and someone tells you how cute your kid is and asks if you're babysitting, say: "Aw, thanks so much. No, I'm not babysitting. I'm his father, so I'm just being a dad, never a babysitter. But again, thank you so much for the kind words and have a great day."

Sure, that might still piss some people off or rub them the wrong way, but there will also be an equal number of people who won't care or who may walk away learning something from your response. I've started some really great conversations that caused people to rethink their words, compared to if I had just nodded and said nothing. Because as much as we all love social media and blasting our opinions into the vastness of the internet, nothing is as effective as face-to-face conversations if you're looking to actually make a difference. And if everyone is having these little conversations, there is a greater potential for us to make a truly large impact.

Finally, by the time my third son was born, my two other sons were old enough to be able to register these conversations in real time and internalize them. If left unchallenged with no pushback, a well-meaning attempt at a compliment that promotes an outdated and harmful worldview would be cemented in the head of an impressionable young man who now thinks that moms should be expected to perform their duties, while dads should be unnecessarily heralded just for showing up. The goal is to model the behavior and lessons you want your children to learn.

PARENTING TIP #10: Avoid stereotypically gendered clothes/products

I am not what you'd call fashionable. An examination of my closet will find that 75 percent of all my shirts feature the New England Patriots or Boston Red Sox, and if I could live my life in jeans and cargo shorts, that'd be ideal. So when it came to dressing my infant son, I figured that as long as he avoided clothing with any New York sports teams, I wouldn't care one bit what he wore.

As usual, I was wrong. It turned out problematic baby clothes soon sent me into a Hulk-rage spiral.

When you have a kid, people buy you all sorts of weird clothing that they think is funny or cute, but most of it just makes you cringe. Like the one from a family member that said: "Lock Up Your Daughters." (See Parenting Tip #1.) Really? That's feeding into the ridiculous male stereotype and declaring that my infant son is inherently incapable of holding back his animalistic impulses to the point that everyone else needs to hide away their daughters lest they become his next victims . . . you can already see just how problematic this "joke" has become. Second, how do you know he's going to go after your daughters? He could very well be gay, so why not lock up your sons? And God help us all if he's bisexual—I guess that'll require a padded room and a Hannibal Lecter mask to keep everyone safe.

Then there was the truly off-putting onesie my wife inexplicably brought home one day that said "Mommy's Little Stud" on the front. Where do I start with that one? If you don't want to go the Oedipal Complex route (and I really, really don't), then you're left with Mom being proud of her son's future sexual conquests, which is just weird. Or she's intending to breed him like a prized canine.

It's no better with clothes for girls, either. In fact, it's probably worse. While shirts marketed for boys tend to talk about being smart and becoming future geniuses, shirts for girls are all about cherries, lollipops, and descriptions of beauty. One especially vile shirt read "I'm too pretty to do homework," and JCPenney was forced to pull it from stores after the justifiable backlash.[17] In 2013, the Children's Place was called out on social media for a girl's shirt that listed "My best subjects," with the boxes "Shopping," "Music," and "Dance" checked off, while "Math" remained unchecked. Or the shirts that read "Smart Like Dad" for boys but "Pretty Like

---

17   Melissa Bell, "JCPenney Pulls 'I'm Too Pretty to Do Homework' Shirt After Online Complaints," *Washington Post*, August 31, 2011, https://www.washingtonpost.com/blogs/blogpost/post/jcpenney-promotes-im-too-pretty-to-do-homework-shirt/2011/08/31/gIQAxFD4rJ_blog.html

Mom" for girls. There are countless other examples but you get the point. Regardless of sex, my main question is: why the hell are we unnecessarily sexualizing infants, and can we please stop this shit yesterday?

All this goes back to an earlier point about how we unthinkingly limit potential and place unnecessary and arbitrary confines on boys and girls. It's not just a shirt, and it's not just a joke when these ideas are being sold to tens of millions of people across the country. When looked at collectively, it shows how boys and girls are being placed in socially and culturally constructed boxes that restrain their identities, self-expression, self-worth, and potential. As parents, we want our kids to think they're capable of doing anything, so please think twice about literally covering kids with garb that holds them down.

Finally, I was pushed over the edge by a onesie my wife took a picture of after Will was born. It said "This shirt is daddy-proof," and it came complete with arrows and labels for its wearer's head, arms, and feet. Get it? Because dads could not figure out how to do baby chores without any help.

I can already hear some of you sighing or see you rolling your eyes; perhaps you think I'm being too sensitive and nitpicky. But honestly, this is just a small representation of a much bigger problem that's far more complicated than it may initially seem. Joking about dads being morons when it comes to parenting sends the message that we have low expectations for fathers. Unfortunately, many guys see the low bar set by society, internalize it, and only rise up high enough to meet the minimum standard. Not only is that bad for dads, it's very harmful to mothers, as well, because that puts the onus on them to pick up the bulk of childcare duties and places a heavier burden that's already disproportionately on their shoulders. Plus, as I've mentioned before, while the baby wearing this onesie obviously can't read yet, their siblings as young as three and four can. And let me tell you something—kids are way smarter and more intuitive than we give them credit for; they will absolutely pick up on this and internalize it in ways you can't imagine.

That's why I'll never for the life of me understand why, even when we know we have a toxic masculinity problem (which includes not enough men thinking that childcare is their job), we intentionally dress our kids up in shirts that exacerbate the problem and further demean and alienate men at the very outset of their manhood journey. Sure, it's a onesie, but small things add up, and every time we buy into this gendered bullshit, we perpetuate the problem and further set ourselves up for failure.

So, don't do it. Don't dress your kids in clothing that denigrates men or women. Don't sexualize infants before they're even able to walk or talk. There are plenty of clothing options that don't involve misogyny, sexism, and anti-dad overtones. And when you not only avoid the problematic ones but also call them out when you see them, you're making a tiny but crucial step in the right direction.

As for the onesie that says "I can't even talk yet but I already hate the Yankees"? That one's OK by me.

PARENTING TIP #11: Parents–don't gatekeep

I'd never heard of the term *maternal gatekeeping* prior to becoming a parent, but it's an important one to discuss because it feeds into toxic masculinity and solidifies problematic gender roles.

According to a study in the *Journal of Marriage and Family*,[18] maternal gatekeeping happens when one person in the

---

18 Sarah M. Allen, Alan J. Hawkins, "Maternal Gatekeeping: Mother's Beliefs and Behaviors That Inhibit Greater Father Involvement in Family Work," *Journal of Marriage and the Family*, February 1999, 199-212.

relationship internalizes all that pressure to be perfect (usually moms) and starts hoarding all parenting duties to make sure every little thing is done the "right way." Unfortunately, the right way becomes code for "*her* way" in heterosexual relationships, and dads often end up feeling ostracized and not included, which causes them to further retreat from the work they should be putting in with their kids. This, in turn, becomes a negative self-fulfilling prophecy as resentment builds up on both sides: the additional hours women spend on caretaking means they are hurt professionally since they're spending fewer hours at work; meanwhile, dads don't see the need or don't have the space to get involved with basic caretaking and household duties.

Sarah Schoppe-Sullivan, a professor of human sciences and psychology at Ohio State University who studies maternal gatekeeping, told *CNN*: "Gatekeeping really seems to depend on how much a woman internalizes societal standards about being a good mom. The more you care about (being viewed as a good mom), the less likely you are to give up control over that domain."[19] It's not just moms, either. A 2017 study published in the *Journal of Family Psychology* found that gay fathers are also likely to fall into gatekeeping tendencies based on societal pressure and judgments regarding being seen as fit parents.[20]

In my experience, this problem presented itself quietly at first, without anyone realizing that anything was wrong. My wife is a fantastic mother who, like the vast majority of moms, feels that everyone, everywhere, is judging them on everything. Even

---

19 Elissa Strauss, "Maternal Gatekeeping: Why Moms Don't Let Dads Help," *CNN*, December 6, 2017, https://www.cnn.com/2017/12/06/health/maternal-gatekeeping-strauss/index.html

20 Kristin Sweeney, Abbie Goldberg, Randi Garcia, "Not a 'Mom Thing': Predictors of Gatekeeping in Same-Sex and Heterosexual Parent Families," *Journal of Family Psychology*, August 2017 Volume 31(5), 521-531.

when you've got an infant, and you can't really be judged because babies don't do much wrong yet, MJ stressed about the one thing that seemed to matter: clothes. I always rolled my eyes when she'd put Will in these fancy matching clothes before she left the house, as if he were some sort of very tiny runway model. But hey, it seemed to make her happy, so I didn't knock it. However, when it was my turn to take the baby out and get him dressed, I did it differently. I was much more functionally minded than fashion forward, which meant colors that didn't always match, stripes and solids going together, and hats that (allegedly) had no business being worn with a nonmatching outfit. My feeling was that as long as our baby was dressed appropriately for the weather, who would give a shit about what he looked like?

Well, my wife did. She gave lots of shits. Whenever I was out with the baby and I sent her pictures, she'd cringe and yell at me for dressing Will "wrong." Then I began to notice that she would lay out Will's clothes ahead of time on the days I was supposed to look after Will solo. When I asked her why, she told me it was because I clearly didn't know how to dress my son properly, so she had to step in and do it for me. I admit, it was insulting because it made me feel dumb and, worst of all, as if my own partner in this whole parenting gig didn't trust me. When I communicated that to MJ, she explained her side of the story and told me about the unique pressures of being a mom that I just couldn't comprehend from where I stood as a man. As a dad, as long as I kept the baby alive, I was hailed as a conquering hero, but if moms take babies out in an outfit that doesn't match or isn't Instagram worthy, they take major heat for it. After we communicated and had a better understanding of where the other was coming from, we compromised and agreed that we'd dress the baby however we saw fit on our respective solo days with no negative feedback from the other. It worked.

But gatekeeping can happen in many other areas, and it has the potential to not only wreak some genuine havoc on relationships, but also influence the children in the relationship who witness it.

Case in point, household chores. If you're a Type A personality (or your partner is one), there can be severe gatekeeping tendencies when it comes to loading the dishwasher, folding the laundry, cooking, or mowing the lawn when one person is constantly "helping" the other person. I'm guilty of it with the lawn because I have a system and a specific way I like it to look, and if MJ tried to do it (which doesn't happen because she's allergic to mown grass), I think I'd have a fit. Conversely, my wife has *very* strong feelings when it comes to how laundry should be folded, and when I attempted to help her in the past, she got so frustrated she actually got hives and then just refolded everything I did after I left.

The truly harmful part is when kids see this happen when they get older, portraying a rigid gender stereotype that will affect their worldview. Based on his parents' habits, my oldest son has always known that men mow the lawn and women do the laundry. So, guess what happened when he turned seven and we started making him do the laundry?

"Why do I have to do it? That's a job for girls, right?"

My wife and I are college-educated, progressive liberals from Massachusetts who care about gender roles and egalitarian parenting, and we still managed to fuck this up and contribute to the very problem we had committed to battle against. It's during moments like this that I'm reminded just how deeply embedded these roles are in our lives and in society, and how easy it is for anyone to fall back into the trap.

The solution to the problem of gatekeeping, I've found, is to let go of the little things and trust that you chose your partner for a reason. So what if the lawn might not be mowed with that cool wave pattern you liked from Pinterest? And does it really matter if the shirts aren't folded precisely in the manner you're accustomed to as long as the laundry is neatly put away? And if the baby is dressed warmly enough for winter or cool enough so as not to sweat to death in the summer heat, does it matter if they're wearing two different socks or stripes together with plaids? No, it doesn't. But what does matter is actively engaging both parents in caretaking and household duties so that one of you isn't left stewing in a vat of resentment; and your kids see the importance of an equal division of labor and a relationship that thrives on reciprocity and mutual respect.

PARENTING TIP #12: Model respect for stay-at-home parents

I love my children wholly and unconditionally and with every fiber of my being. I love them in a way that brings me to my knees at the very thought of the enormity and the expanse of my love for the three little lives I have created, and nothing brings me more joy than spending quality time with them.

But I would never be a full-time stay-at-home dad. No fucking way, no how. I'm just not built for it, and I'd lose my damn mind if I were solely responsible for the day-in, day-out, twenty-four-seven caretaking of my three boys. I enjoy my job too much to give it up, and my kids wouldn't be getting the best of me if they got 100 percent of me 100 percent of the time.

I guess that's why I have so much love and respect for the stay-at-home parents out there who are doing what I could never do. And while I wouldn't go as far as to say it's the "toughest job in the world" (because, hey, you're not mining coal and you can wear your pajamas), I do think it's the most *important* job around, and that's why I never fail to value what my wife does on a daily basis. I acknowledge her work (yes, it is work), I thank her for what she does, and I make damn sure to do it in front of the kids.

Of course, that's what I do now. But how we got from then to now is a different story.

One day, shortly after we moved into our new house, I remember feeling extraordinarily frustrated with life. I was busting my ass at work trying to get a promotion that would allow us to better afford our modest piece of the American Dream out in suburbia, and I felt like I wasn't getting far enough fast enough. While I believed I was maintaining an impenetrable firewall between my frustration at work and my home life, that simply wasn't the case. I distinctly remember coming home from a long day at the office for three days in a row and seeing the same dirty dishes in the sink. That led to some comments about said dishes, which I thought were very sly and coded. I offered to do them but was told by my wife that she'd get to them soon. Three days isn't "soon" in my book, though, and finally, on day four, I had had enough. I brought it up (in what I thought was a gentle and nonsexist way) by reminding her that we all have jobs to do, and that this was hers since she was home the most, and that I didn't think it was asking too much that the dishes be done after three days. I covered my bases by assuring her that if it were me staying home full-time and I had let things go, she'd have every right to criticize me, as well.

It was at that moment when my then-four-year-old middle child, who I didn't even realize had been listening, chimed in and gave me a reality slap. "Dads work hard and make money to buy us things," he said, wagging a finger at my wife. "Moms stay home to clean and fold laundry."

Fuck.

I immediately apologized to my wife for being a dick, and then I had a long talk with Sam about gender roles and how Daddy had messed up by talking to Mom in that way. Because what I hadn't taken the time to know, before I launched into my lecture about the dishes, was that Will was coming home from school every day in tears, anxious about moving to a new town and having to make new friends; that he was taking out his aggression on Sam and bullying him relentlessly; that Sam was internalizing all that hostility and taking it out on my wife by throwing epic tantrums and physically accosting her (we'd later learn that Sam has ADHD and Opposition Defiant Disorder). The reason MJ hadn't told me all this, either, was because she knew how difficult my work had been and was trying to keep the "extraneous" stuff from me, at least temporarily, so I could focus. With all these pressures on her, something had to give, and this time it was the dishes. And there I was, giving her a ration of shit for it while simultaneously conveying to my sons that men work and provide while women take care of the home.

Although MJ hasn't worked outside the home in roughly a decade, I sat my children down and talked to them about her former career. They were shocked to learn that she was a top-performing bank manager for Bank of America and then Citizens—a valued employee so talented and hardworking that she routinely earned free trips to places like the Bahamas and Arizona, where I would accompany her as a freeloading husband, whose salary was dwarfed by what she took home at the time. My children had no idea about their mom's working past because I had never thought to bring it up, so their entire view of parenting was men at work, women at home.

Talk openly with your kids about the value of at-home parents, and show your gratitude on days other than Mother's Day or Father's Day. Find age-appropriate ways to convey to kids that parenting is hard work and that at-home parents are worth their weight in gold, often taking up a much more difficult job than parents who work "offsite" at an office. This will help create a more nuanced understanding of and appreciation for both dads and moms who take on these roles.

PARENTING TIP #13: Embrace and encourage stay-at-home dads, and make sure your kids do, too

The good news is that stay-at-home moms tend to get a lot of credit for what they do, as they should. Generally speaking, when a woman is asked what she does and she says, "I'm a full-time stay-at-home mom," the reaction is most likely a positive one. It's a role women have cultivated for a long time, and society is used to seeing and accepting them as primary caretakers.

But that's not the case for men who choose to be full-time at-home dads. Despite a Pew Research study that shows there are two million stay-at-home dads in America, a number that nearly doubled from 1989 to 2012,[21] at-home men still face a ton of problematic behavior from all corners of society. Mainly because of toxic masculinity and rigid gender stereotypes, most people still believe that a man's job is to be out of the house and earning a paycheck, bringing home the proverbial bacon, and being a financial provider who allows his wife not to work so she can stay home with the kids.

---

21 "Rising Number of Stay-at-Home Dads," *Pew Research Center*, June 15, 2016, https://www.pewresearch.org/fact-tank/2019/06/12/fathers-day-facts/ft_16-06-14_fathersday_stayathomerising/

Through my work as a parent blogger, my network includes hundreds, if not thousands, of stay-at-home dads. I follow the National At-Home Dad Network (athomedad.org) closely, and in my conversations with these men over the years, I've found that they are often treated with unnecessary bias, distrust, and even contempt from men and women alike (proving that toxic masculinity is not a problem restricted only to men).

It's well known that most of the parents who show up at school drop-offs and pick-ups and who volunteer in classrooms are women. So when men appear in these spaces, they're greeted with comments like "Oh look, daddy has the day off" and "That's nice that mommy gets a break," comments that subscribe to the same harmful men-at-work and women-at-home stereotype.

Even worse than being on the receiving end of such comments is navigating the playdates (or lack thereof) when you're a stay-at-home dad. When full-time at-home dads take their children to the playground and join parenting networking groups, like moms, they often report facing the cold shoulder from fellow parents or even outright ostracization. Why? For far too many people, the sight of a grown man around small children automatically brings to mind a child molester or pedophile (which, unfortunately, is not hyperbole or an overreaction). Even so, there are many dads who are just trying to find a supportive parenting community and who end up being the only man in attendance, while facing an inherent distrust, because *why isn't that man at work where he belongs?! What are his intentions?*

It is very common for parents who know each other through parenting groups or daycare or preschool to schedule playdates at a park or at someone's house to get additional social interactions in for their little ones. I've seen this happen over and over again as a regular, everyday occurrence among women, with no issues or worries whatsoever. However, inviting a man to a play-date becomes a completely different story. Stay-at-home dad after stay-at-home dad has reported being left out of the playdate circle because either the organizing mom in question didn't feel comfortable hanging out with a man, or her husband flatly forbade it. (Guys, are you really dictating who your wives can and can't hang out with just because you're insecure? If you don't trust your wife enough to have an innocent playdate with a fellow parent, you have far more to worry about than just a playdate.) Keep in mind that these are fathers who are bringing their babies and toddlers over for structured play; it isn't a polyamorous key party, and despite what society keeps trying to tell us, we men aren't walking erections looking for a place to land—especially while we're with our damn children. Yet that's precisely how we're perceived—see? That's how seemingly innocuous stereotypes can transform into something more harmful—and it really sucks that our kids have to suffer because toxic masculinity defines all men as sexual predators just waiting for an opportunity to pounce.

I'm a dad who routinely took his kids to playgrounds—and holy shit, is that a minefield for dads. The vast majority of the time, I was the only dad in a sea of moms, and the side-eye I received was legendary. The moms would watch me warily as they tried to figure out if any of the children were mine or if I was some sketchy pervert trying to take pictures of their kids. Once, I learned a very hard lesson when a kid on the playground climbed too high on the jungle gym. Afraid, he started calling for his mom, who couldn't hear him because she was on the phone. Being a dad, I went up and asked him if he'd like my help getting down. He said yes, and so I picked him up by the waist and lowered him to safety on the mulch below. Well, all this mom saw was a strange man reaching up to grab her kid, and did I get an earful from her as she came over screaming and threatening to call the police. The truth is, I'm certain that if it had been another mother helping her kid, Cell Phone Mom probably wouldn't have batted an eyelash; she might even have thanked her! What happened that day left an indelible mark on me, and not for the better—it taught me not to help other kids I don't know unless they're truly in physical danger. But that's the predicament we're in when we live in a society mired with rigid gender stereotypes.

Of course, it's not just mothers who hold on to antiquated thoughts when it comes to stay-at-home dads. There is no shortage of alpha male morons who never fail to snicker or greet with outright scorn the men who stay at home full time with their kids. These tend to be the men whose values are directly tied to their paychecks and their job titles, the ones who say to at-home dads, "Wow, well, I'd like a vacation, too," and "Isn't it embarrassing for you to let your wife make all the money?", nevermind that a stay-at-home dad has actively chosen to spend his resources and time on caring about the most precious people in his life. These are the men who joke about "sugar mamas" and openly wonder if full-time fathers have "manginas," while labeling them "betas." Like Donald Trump, they brag about having never changed a diaper,[22] as if being uninvolved is something to which one should aspire. They're so stuck in the toxic-masculinity mud that they don't realize there's nothing more masculine than dedicating yourself to the positive upbringing of the next generation.

---

22 Andrew Kaczynski, Megan Apper, "Donald Trump Thinks Men Who Change Diapers Are Acting 'Like the Wife'," Buzzfeed, April 24, 2016, https://www.buzzfeednews.com/article/andrewkaczynski/donald-trump-thinks-men-who-change-diapers-are-acting-like-t

This kind of parental alienation toward stay-at-home dads isn't just limited to "in real life" scenarios; it happens online as well.

When I first became a dad in 2007, my wife and I briefly discussed me staying home full-time with the baby because MJ made more than double my salary, and daycare was really expensive in Massachusetts. But I wanted to talk to people in a similar boat who could relate to everything going on in my life before we made a decision. The only thing I could really find at the time were the birth groups at BabyCenter.com, essentially an online bulletin board where people could talk about whatever topics they wanted, and where you were split up into the months you were expecting. My group was April 2008, and it consisted of all women.

Never one to be shy, I immediately began to immerse myself in the group, offer opinions, and ask questions. And while some of the women were very welcoming (in fact, I still talk to them today), a few were not. At all. To the point that they discussed holding a referendum on whether I, as a man, should even be allowed in a group they assumed to be solely for women. Apparently, men weren't supposed to be in this realm, and it actually got to the point where they considered kicking me out. If this was supposed to be a group made up of likeminded people sharing the common experience of parenthood, why didn't I belong?

If toxic masculinity promotes the lie that men work while women stay home to look after the kids, it's no wonder that women, too, buy into this ingrained cultural myth. I have personally experienced many women doubting the ability and fitness of men to parent, and the irony of moms calling for more involvement from dads, but then isolating and alienating them whenever they did step up, was never lost on me.

Which leads me to my final playground story. Though more subtle than the previous incident, in which I almost had the police called on me for being a suspected deviant, the familiar trademarks of toxic masculinity were equally insidious. The playground by our house has a plastic climbing structure that really tested Will's abilities. It starts off vertical with holes for hands and feet, before twisting down horizontally and then back up again to reach the platform on the other side. I liked it because it not only forced Will to think in advance about where to put his hands and feet, it also necessitated strategic decisions regarding whether he wanted to traverse it via the top or the bottom. He must have tried two dozen times and failed spectacularly, falling to the mulch floor below, only to dust himself off and try again. Once when we were trying out the structure, I noticed a helicopter mom on the playground who winced disapprovingly every time Will fell off. At one point, Will slipped but caught himself, and he was hanging there, trying to regain his footing, when Ms. Helicopter Mom, who had clearly had enough, came running over, saying, "Here, let me help you, sweetie."

I was right there. Me, his dad. Watching and voicing my support for him but refusing to help because I knew that he could do it himself and that he was in no danger. But here was a woman who thought so little of me that she didn't hesitate to correct my parenting choices in my presence, even though it was none of her business. My blood was boiling, but I calmly told her that I was his dad and that I had everything under control. She wouldn't relent and told me in no uncertain terms that my son clearly needed help that I wasn't giving him. Finally, Will came through for me when he said, "No thanks, I can do it myself." And then he did. And then I gloated. (Because I'm petty like that.)

In closing, please don't alienate or belittle stay-at-home dads. They are the ones who are most eagerly taking up the call of involved parenthood, and they need your support, not your scorn or distrust. And when your kids see more men actively caring for and participating in the upbringing of children, the next generation will see it as the norm, not a novelty.

Chapter 3

Don't Let School Harden Boys Unnecessarily

A S A PARENT, YOU SPEND THE FIRST YEAR JUST TRYING TO KEEP them alive; then you simply hope to survive the Terrible Twos and Threes; and as they get a little older and are able to better understand age-appropriate lessons, you start to do what you can to implement solid values. You're amazed as you see daily progress, and you realize they're truly starting to comprehend your lessons (instead of just repeating them back to you). These are early lessons that will set the framework for how you'll eventually discuss the complexities of race, misogyny, homophobia, transphobia, consent, and every other topic you might be apprehensive about but are necessary to discuss if you want to shape your child into becoming a functional and respectful member of society.

Well, I hate to break it to you, but the bad news is all that progress and all those advancements you make while they're in controlled social circles? So much of it is going to go up in smoke once school starts and your kid is exposed to all the other children with parents whose own unique views are directly parroted to their kids. Basically, you'll lose a shit ton of control when school starts and the opinions of your kids' friends begin to hold a lot more sway and influence than dear old Mom's and Dad's.

That doesn't mean you give up. It just means you need to be prepared to put all these lessons on repeat and to work tirelessly to battle stereotypes involving toxic masculinity with your children, because I can guarantee you one thing for certain: they're coming, and coming fast.

PARENTING TIP #14: Teach kids to embrace differences, not fear or mock them

October 22, 2018, started out like every other day. I woke up, took the train to work, and went about my day. But less than twenty-four hours later, I'd find myself (and my middle son, Sam) in the middle of an intense media and social media storm centering around toxic masculinity to the tune of eighty-thousand-plus likes on Twitter, a host of national and international media coverage, and eventually an appearance on the Today Show.

And even though that moment yielded me this book deal, I'd gladly trade it all in if it meant Sammy would not have had to go through what he had endured.

If you didn't catch our story in the media or on Twitter, Sam was ridiculed by his fellow kindergarten students for wearing nail polish. It was surprising because it wasn't the first time Sam had worn his brightly colored nails to school in Massachusetts, where people are generally more progressive. His grandmother, my mom, is a former manicurist, and she's been painting his nails since he was in preschool with no one ever uttering so much as a cross word. Sam is a fireworks show of a human being, and he burns bright and loud in everything he does, so it came as no surprise to me that he was drawn to fire-engine-red nail polish. And since we never made a big deal out of it, Sam had not a single inkling that anyone anywhere could possibly have a problem with a boy wearing nail polish out in public.

My wife called me at work that day, and I could hear Sam wailing in the background. This, in and of itself, wasn't surprising because Sam has pretty severe ADHD and Opposition Defiant Disorder, so I just figured that he had a bad day and was melting down. But MJ told me he was crying so hard that she couldn't coax out of him what was wrong, so I got on the phone and calmed him down until he was able to tell us what happened.

Turns out, what happened was a whole bunch of toxic masculinity bullshit that had crushed my little boy. We learned that Sam had been confronted by most of the boys and girls in his kindergarten class throughout the day, who told him repeatedly and forcefully that he needed to take his nail polish off right away. Why? Because boys don't wear nail polish. Because nail polish is only for girls, and boys shouldn't be allowed to wear girl things to class (or anywhere else). Sam was cast as a boy who had failed to live up to masculine ideals. And make no mistake, it wasn't just the boys who teased Sam. In fact, most of his tormentors were girls—because the trap of toxic masculinity impacts every single last one of us. While these kids weren't physically threatening, they were relentless in their declarations of what was acceptable for boys, despite Sam's protestations and desperate pleas to convince them of all the lessons we had taught him about acceptance, tolerance, and giving the finger to gender norms. We teach our kids to try to work out their problems with other kids as long as they aren't in danger, which is why he didn't tell his teacher (who is outstanding and would've absolutely stopped that shit in its tracks) what was happening. The end result was Sam getting an earful in bursts all day long at lunch, recess, and during breaks in classroom instruction, until he finally just collapsed when MJ picked him up from school.

I was fucking furious.

First of all, it's the absolute toughest part of parenting to watch your kids get picked on like that. Second, I was less angry with the kids and more pissed at their parents, because five-year-olds aren't naturally discriminatory and close-minded. That shit is learned—from society, from media, and most of all from parents and guardians who hold those views themselves and filter it down to their kids. Most of all, I was incensed because Sam was now asking us to clean off the nail polish in order to put an end to the bullying. We asked him if he still liked the nail polish, and he said yes. We asked him if he'd keep wearing it if no one was making fun of him, and he said yes again. Here was an open-minded kid who had been taught the virtues of "to each their own," and all it took was one day at kindergarten for him to be beaten into submission.

We tried talking to him that night. We told him it was important to do what made him happy no matter the consequences. We told him the other kids had just gotten some bad advice from other people, but that they could learn the same positive lessons he did if he continued wearing his nail polish. We also pointed out all the other men in society who wear nail polish that he might admire, although all he was really interested in was knowing if his favorite football player of all time, New England Patriots tight end Rob Gronkowski, wore nail polish. I couldn't confirm an instance of Gronk wearing polish, but I told a white lie and let Sam know that Gronk was a fellow polisher. And then MJ and I begged him to at least keep his nails painted overnight and consider wearing it back to school, but if he still felt the same way in the morning, of course we'd take it off. He agreed to that deal.

Just before he went to bed, my oldest son, Will, had the best idea ever, and one I was ashamed for not having right away: Will asked me to paint his fingernails in solidarity with his brother to show off at school the next day. Suddenly, I was having trouble seeing through the tears. Needless to say, I loved the idea and painted my nails as well, wearing them to work the next day. Despite their near constant sibling bickering, Will was the first one to jump to Sam's defense, which made an enormous difference for Sam. Having backup and strength in numbers always does the trick.

After Sam went to bed, I unleashed all of my fury in a rant that I turned into a Twitter thread. It mentioned what happened and cast Sam as a cautionary tale of how quickly and deeply toxic masculinity negatively impacts people. I secured my wife's permission to post and hit publish shortly before turning in for bed. I had no idea what I was in for when I awoke the next day.

At first glance, I thought my phone was broken. The buzzing was constant and the notifications were coming so fast I just figured there was some kind of glitch. As I wiped the sleep away, my eyes suddenly went wide when I saw thousands upon thousands of likes, retweets, and replies. I tapped MJ on the shoulder to wake her and simply said, "Oh fuck," because I had gone viral before and had been exposed to the seedy underbelly of Twitter, otherwise known as the troll dungeon. I know what it's like to have thousands of strangers crawling your accounts and pulling photos of your family to turn into memes. I remember all too well the stinging criticisms and never-ending torrent of abuse from people who think you're turning your child into a "bitch" or a "cuck." And I remember the sick feeling that occurred when those zealots found my parents' phone number, called them, excoriated them for raising such a terrible human being, and then threatened my safety. All of which is part and parcel of toxic masculinity. It's not enough to disagree with someone; you need to threaten them. Intimidate them. Insult their manhood. And then threaten physical violence. Needless to say, I was immediately fearful of a repeat performance.

And make no mistake, that happened to an extent. My Twitter thread surged and surged, and soon media outlets were calling. *People Magazine, The Guardian, Mashable, Good Morning America, BBC,* and so many more all published positive articles about Sam, which propelled the issue even further into the limelight and immediately attracted the expected backlash. Some of the responses included comments like "I am not shocked at all that his dad is a fat bitch. I feel sorry for the kid" and "Just because you have #lowT (testosterone) doesn't mean you need to make you [sic] boy into a sissy bitch. It's ok for men to be men and women to be women, just like Fords and Dodges are different."

But the pièce de résistance was making the front page of the *Daily Stormer.* If you're lucky enough not to know what it is, it's a notorious American neo-Nazi, white supremacist, and Holocaust denial commentary and message board website that advocates for the genocide of Jews and considers itself part of the alt-right movement. I know people say that all publicity is good publicity, but those people probably haven't woken up to find their picture, as well as photos of their beautiful children, up on a legitimate Nazi website, where they are being torn apart in the worst possible way by the worst possible people on the planet. Imagine, for a second, having to tell your wife that you and your five-year-old are currently being featured and analyzed by actual Nazis.

I won't lie, I considered pulling the plug immediately. But once I stopped focusing on the negatives, I realized something extraordinary. The responses were overwhelmingly in support of Sam! In addition to people simply offering words of support, we began receiving pictures of other boys who love wearing nail polish and who had faced adversity because of it. Then we started getting pictures and stories from men of all ages in locations from all over the world who regularly paint their fingernails and toenails, all urging Sam to keep being himself.

A man in Scotland named Charlie took time out of his day to send a video of himself, with his nails painted, thanking Sam for inspiring him to paint his nails and reassuring him that being true to oneself is what makes a man admirable. Mothers and fathers wrote me emails and even asked to reach out on Facebook Messenger to give me heart-wrenching and tearful accounts of watching their own sons go through similar situations, and it broke my heart. While some of the children had the support and resolve to give their critics the middle finger, others felt the crushing weight of the pressure and ultimately stopped painting their nails. They hid who they were deep down and stopped being themselves, simply because the daily torment was too much. Now here were their parents, turning to a stranger on the internet, asking for help on how to fix the problem. Except I didn't have the answers. But what I learned is that a huge part of the solution is in support and outreach. (More on that in a bit.)

Then came support from businesses like OPI, which sent Sam a ton of nail polish in the mail, as well as Jin Soon, which ended up naming one of their nail polish colors in honor of Sam. People at companies all over the globe were painting their nails and sending out pictures supporting Sam from their corporate Twitter handles. Celebrities like former Patriots player Martellus Bennett and famed voice actress Tara Strong also personally reached out. Then came the most amazing thing: Rob Gronkowski recorded a video personally addressing Sam to encourage him to keep being himself, which was tweeted out by the official Patriots Twitter account. Something that, to this psychotic, lifelong Patriots fan, meant so much that I really can't adequately describe it.

It was the overwhelming support that next morning that will always stay with me, and it was directly responsible for Sam bravely choosing to continue to wear his painted nails to school that next day. As I sat with him in the predawn darkness getting ready for work and scrolled through the endless stream of messages and pictures of boys and men having the courage to flip the bird to toxic masculinity, his smile grew wider and his confidence expanded exponentially. For one glorious moment, Twitter and social media worked as I believe it is intended to work—a global community of people finding common ground and reaching out from all corners of the world to support a bullied boy in the face of adversity. Having been through the social media wringer several times over the course of my adult life, I won't pretend for a second that social media and the way certain platforms are regulated don't come with major warts and beyond-problematic policies; but in this case, positivity won out because people proved they are mostly good and are willing to share that goodness with the world.

Which leads directly to my next tip.

PARENTING TIP #15: Teach boys to stand up for what's right

One child in Sam's class stood up for him during the nail polish incident. Just one. It's not like Sam doesn't have friends—he's a well-liked kid who does well in school and gets along with his classmates. But Sam learned a hard lesson that day, which is that even preexisting friendships aren't enough if you're suddenly different from the group and the subject of scorn. If you run afoul of tried and true gender norms that upset the generally accepted balance, those friendships can dissipate faster than Donald Trump's train of thought when the teleprompter malfunctions. They either stand idly by while the teasing happens, thankful it's not them in the crosshairs, or worse, they join the crowd and turn on you.

One of the silver linings of the whole fingernail fiasco for me was being able to personally thank the little boy in Sam's class who bravely stood by his side. I was also able to thank his parents for raising the kind of kid who thinks for himself and who stands up for others when they need it. Make no mistake, of all the remedies and potential fixes to bullying, this is by far the most effective and impactful. But since it involves placing yourself in harm's way and potentially being the subject of scorn and derision as well, it's also the most difficult. Yet this boy did exactly that, and his support gave Sam a glimmer of hope and a small but hugely important respite and oasis during the storm.

As a parent, that's the kind of kid I'm trying to raise. It's the kind of kid we should *all* try to raise. When that family came to our house for Halloween trick-or-treating, it was all I could do not to hug them on the spot as the tears welled up in my eyes. I thanked them and let them know that their son's conscientiousness and moral compass will end up making a positive difference in this world.

Once one little seed of kindness and bravery is planted, it will snowball. That boy stood up for Sam in class, I wrote the Twitter thread, my oldest son heroically decided to wear painted nails to school the next day, and by the end of the week, guess what happened? Some wonderful soul I still haven't been able to identify had an idea that everyone in our public school system would paint their fingernails that Friday, not only in honor of Sam, but also to show support for everyone in the community who doesn't conform to traditional gender stereotypes. That, combined with his teachers turning what had happened into a learning opportunity for students, allowed us to reach a tipping point where Sam was no longer an outcast; he was now a celebrity. Suddenly, it was cool to be different, and there was a feeling of a protective wall that had formed around Sam. Once it was framed in a more positive way, kids were clamoring to be a living, breathing security blanket for Sam and others like him. When the news crews came to do a story at the school, there was no shortage of boys clad in bright nail polish lining up to talk about how this was no big deal and even how they liked doing this kind of "girl" stuff in the privacy of their own homes but were now grateful they could be a little more open with it after the story broke.

If you give boys just a little bit of leeway and show them that they have support, you'll be shocked at how quickly and eagerly they'll explore outside of their narrowly defined "masculine" worlds. The only way that can happen is through strength in numbers, when kids band together and stand up for what's right. That is unbelievably difficult and much easier said than done, but it truly is the antidote to fixing the problem. And all this starts with parents who raise kids to stand up and put themselves in the proverbial line of fire when it comes to bullying.

So, moms and dads, teach boys to walk their own path and stand up for others. Sam's nail polish incident showed me it's possible for kids to do the right thing if they feel empowered and if they're shown how to be leaders who strive to be on the right side of inclusiveness. But parents need to show them the road map and model that behavior so it's easier for them to find their way and emulate. Is it difficult? Absolutely. But the sooner more kids start learning how to do the hard work of standing up for what's right no matter what, the faster society will reach a juncture where fewer kids will have to take this kind of a stand because more kids will know right from wrong.

PARENTING TIP #16: Teach boys that "gay" is not an insult

Care to guess what the number one insult was during Sam's nail polish adventure on social media? That he was "gay." A "fag." A "homo." A "femme" and "transvestite in training." A "pansy" whose dad never taught him to be a real man, which is why he gravitated toward nail polish. And if you've grown up male in this society, these responses should come as no surprise at all.

Let's get this out in the open right now so there is no confusion: I was very guilty of this in the past. My formative years in the late eighties and early nineties were filled with homophobia that I didn't even realize at the time was homophobia. Everything we didn't like was simply termed *gay*. Someone had a dumb idea? It was gay. Someone was being an idiot? Don't be gay. And this is from someone who grew up with gay aunts and who went to Provincetown every summer and thinking nothing of men in leather who wandered the streets to their heart's content. I grew up loving many gay people and supporting them at every turn, but that's how deeply ingrained this shit is. When I was finally called out on it, I was legitimately shocked and, frankly, angry that someone would accuse me of homophobia. I tried to explain myself: "When I say *gay*, I don't mean *gay* gay, I just mean *gay* like it's dumb or bad." It took actually hearing the words escape from my mouth to realize the problem. And let me tell you, realizing you're part of the problem you thought you were fighting against is a real mindfuck that leaves you feeling incredibly stupid. Using *gay* as a derogatory term is always wrong, always homophobic, and always fraught with disaster. This is especially true if it is heard by young people who might not be out of the closet yet and who, like most other kids their age, are still struggling to find their community despite knowing they're different.

Unfortunately, it continued even into my twenties. When Will was a newborn baby, I had a visceral, negative reaction to my wife putting him in pink socks. I tried to blame it on gender confusion, but the brutal truth was I was afraid people would call him gay. It took me an embarrassingly long time to realize how much harm my words and thoughts were inflicting on others, that I was subconsciously putting gay men into a separate category distinct from the larger group of "regular" men. In my narrow little universe, which I had erroneously framed as an accepting and nonjudgmental one, I believed that there was no opportunity for gay men to be "real men."

When I think of the number of times I called people, ideas, or things *gay*, I cringe, not only because it was homophobic, but also because I'm 100 percent positive that someone who had been in earshot of me was gay or trans. I try to imagine being them and feeling "othered" on a twenty-four-seven basis. Gay marriage wasn't legal when I was growing up, so they knew the law would treat them as second-class citizens. Since most religions cast homosexuality as a sin, they knew they couldn't even turn to God in all of their confusion and heartache. And with stories like Matthew Shepard's in the news, the University of Wyoming student who was viciously murdered in 1998 because he was gay, I believe they also felt like their very physical safety was threatened. What does it mean, then, for them to hang out with friends who are supposed to love and accept them, except to hear nothing but *gay* being used as a pejorative? As something bad? Something to be avoided? I am forever ashamed that I contributed to the problem instead of being a resource or outlet for friends potentially struggling with their sexuality.

According to The Trevor Project, suicide is the second leading cause of death among young people ages ten to twenty-four, with LGB youth contemplating suicide at almost three times the rate of heterosexuals, while being five times as likely to have actually attempted suicide compared to their heterosexual peers.[23] All parents, regardless of religion or personal beliefs involving the LGBTQ+ community, must be cognizant of their language, because kids who identify as being part of that community are listening to you and the words you choose to use. Remember: there are at-risk kids out there who are shunned by too many in our society and who are looking for a place of shelter and someone who will offer some kind of acceptance. They've experienced shame and ostracization, even if of the unintentional variety, from too many people. The very least we can do, as parents, is use inclusive language and eliminate problematic vocabulary so we're not potentially endangering someone's life.

Case in point: Leelah Alcorn. Born Joshua Alcorn, Leelah was a transgender kid from Ohio who came out to her classmates without issue in 2014. However, she was not accepted by her parents. Actually, that's an understatement: her parents not only didn't accept her, they also isolated her and then tried to "fix" her. They took her to Christian therapists who did not believe that God looked kindly on boys who knew they were girls. When this "therapy" wasn't working, Leelah's parents did something truly unconscionable: they took away her phone and internet access, thereby cutting her off from her friends who

---

23 "Facts About Suicide," The Trevor Project, accessed September 15, 2019, https://www.thetrevorproject.org/resources/preventing-suicide/facts-about-suicide/

were the only lifeline and source of positivity she had. Leelah ended her life by walking in front of a tractor-trailer in December 2014, but not before she explained on Tumblr exactly why she did what she did.

> When I was 14, I learned what transgender meant and cried of happiness. After 10 years of confusion I finally understood who I was. I immediately told my mom, and she reacted extremely negatively, telling me that it was a phase, that I would never truly be a girl, that God doesn't make mistakes, that I am wrong. If you are reading this, parents, please don't tell this to your kids. Even if you are Christian or are against transgender people don't ever say that to someone, especially your kid. That won't do anything but make them hate them self [sic]. That's exactly what it did to me. My mom started taking me to a therapist, but would only take me to christian therapists, (who were all very biased) so I never actually got the therapy I needed to cure me of my depression. I only got more christians telling me that I was selfish and wrong and that I should look to God for help.[24]

A parent's primary job is to love their children unconditionally. I don't care about your religion, your personal philosophy on life, or any of that nonsense. Parents are supposed to love their kids no matter what. They're supposed to be the everlasting and eternal safe space where kids know fully well that they can find the support and comfort they need to get through the hard

---

24 Gillian Mohney, "Leelah Alcorn: Trangender Teen's Reported Suicide Note Makes Dramatic Appeal," *ABC News*, December 31, 2014, https://abcnews.go.com/US/leelah-alcorn-transgender-teens-reported-suicide-note-makes/story?id=27912326

times. If you're a parent who abandons your kid just because your little boy wants to be a girl, that is a disgusting betrayal of the highest order. And in cases like Leelah's, it's nothing short of a death sentence. I have to imagine it's hell on earth knowing that you were part of the reason your child removed themselves from the planet. Don't let homophobic or transphobic behaviors result in the death of a child and a lifetime of regret.

Parents, you don't even have to fully understand or agree with what your child is going through for you to continue loving them. It's a tough situation, and for many, acceptance will not come in the blink of an eye. But you can talk the issue out with your kids, as long as your foundation is one of love and trust as opposed to religious condemnation, judgment, and rejection of the life you had created and that you should be protecting.

Leelah continues:

The only way I will rest in peace is if one day transgender people aren't treated the way I was, they're treated like humans, with valid feelings and human rights. Gender needs to be taught about in schools, the earlier the better. My death needs to mean something. My death needs to be counted in the number of transgender people who commit suicide this year. I want someone to look at that number and say 'that's fuck [sic] up' and fix it. Fix society. Please.

It is not just enough to be careful with the words you use in real life. The fact is, the internet and social media can play a huge role in adding to the problem. That's why I monitor my oldest son's Fortnite playing, texting, and Instagram use because homophobic and toxic language is rampant there. (I use the Bark app, which is a huge help as it flags problematic language on your

child's device and notifies you of slurs, self-harm, bullying, etc.)
Even boys who have impeccable manners in public and who have
parents on the lookout for such things can sink into the swamp
waters of toxic masculinity when no one is watching or listening. My son has had some tough and uncomfortable conversations with good friends about this very topic, while I've had the
same talks with their parents. There's a lot of "boys will be boys"
and "I said the same things when I was a kid" that emerge as
excuses from those conversations, but that shouldn't fly because
we should always want to do better, and not just the bare minimum, for our kids. For example, just because your parents didn't
have you in a car seat and you managed to survive doesn't mean
we shouldn't take advantage of new research and technology to
make our own kids safer. Many men thought nothing of slapping
their secretaries on the ass in the 1950s and 1960s, but we know
that is sexual misconduct and horribly abusive behavior that we
will not stand for today. The same goes for the language we use,
and homophobic phrases like "that's gay" or saying "no homo"
after giving a compliment to another guy—it's harmful, and we
know better. It's simply something we should not do.

On my oldest son's last day of school one year, everyone had
to dress up for the graduation ceremony. One of his male friends
wore a striking pink shirt, and he looked really great and well put
together. I immediately called out to him and told him I loved
the new look; I was impressed that he was wearing such a bold
color and wanted to make sure he felt supported. But before I
could finish telling him how much I liked his outfit, he cut me
off and said, "It's not pink!" No one had even mentioned the
color; that's just where his head was at. I sighed and told him
that pink is not strictly for girls and that it isn't "gay," but I could
tell it wasn't landing. I knew exactly where he had heard that

shit, and I knew he'd hear it again and again. And I died a little inside, because he's a good kid who is simply caught up in a cycle of gendered fuckery that he'll most likely pass on to his own kids.

I understand a lot of this is unintentional and caused by otherwise well-meaning people who simply don't realize the potential negative consequences of their language. That's why I hope the people who see themselves in these examples will have the guts to own up to their behavior and change their ways—good people make mistakes, and we can learn from them. We can't erase the past, but parents have a responsibility to improve the future via our kids and model appropriate language. That needs to be our highest priority, because when it comes to this issue, it's not hyperbole to say it's a matter of life and death.

PARENTING TIP #17: Teach boys that "girl" is not an insult

If referring to something you don't like as "gay" is the number one insult for boys, it's followed closely when someone uses "girl" in a derogatory sense.

Again, I am complicit in this problem. For one of Will's first Christmases, my wife got him a toy kitchen set, which was a secret she also kept from me—and I quickly saw the reason why. I am not a poker player, and my face told the true story of how much I didn't like the idea of my masculine, rough-and-tumble son playing in the kitchen with what was clearly (in my mind) a toy for girls. And I *knew*, even as I was feeling these emotions, that I was wrong to feel that way. But I couldn't help it nor hide it—that's how deeply ingrained toxic masculinity is in all of us. Despite trying my best to be an open-minded dad who doesn't let gender roles pigeonhole my kids or my thinking, there I was, face-to-face with my own biases and bullshit that was holding me back. Of course, the kitchen stayed, and we cooked many an imaginary meal there, but I first had to own up to my initial reaction and actively work to get past it.

For many men, being described as "girly" is a cardinal sin that must be avoided at all costs. Crying too much? Don't be such a girl. Not throwing the ball far or hard enough? Try harder, Sally. Screaming because you're scared of something? Man up and don't be a sissy. These are things every American boy has heard at some point in his life—and internalized, as well. It doesn't even make any sense, to be honest. Who decided that pink = feminine = weak? Who made the judgment that dance = girly/gay = bad? These are artificial cultural constructs that literally have no meaning, yet men have been ruled by these unwritten edicts for years to the point that they now tie themselves into emotional knots rather than live their own truths. I know some great basketball players who took dance classes so they could strengthen their leg muscles and jump higher, and who thought that dance was far more strenuous than practices on the court. Yet, they did so in secret because they were convinced that dancing is "gay" for men and therefore bad. It's maddening and confusing beyond words.

When you constantly send a message to boys that everything involving girls or anything remotely feminine is bad, you're sending a powerful message. And it's certainly not a positive one. Each one of those comments, while seemingly small, add up quickly. For eons, we've told our boys that what we define as feminine equates to something that is bad. Weak. Less than. Perhaps the intent is to use this as motivation to get our boys to try harder and do better, but I've never understood why we need to tear women down and perpetuate gender inequality in order to achieve that goal. Men are the dominant sex in most cultures and civilizations, each of which have seen shameful and unequal treatment of women throughout human history. So, it's not surprising that many men just revert to this language as the default, because the chilling truth is too many men don't have the tools to convey our points in any other way.

But beyond that, these instructions don't even make sense. When a boy gets emotional and expresses those feelings outwardly, we tell him to stop being such a girl. But what is wrong with openly and freely expressing emotion? Women tend to be better communicators precisely because they are allowed by society the leeway to actually express their emotions. This is a good thing. This is something our boys should be encouraged to do and explore. But no, that's too girly, so instead we tell our boys to stuff all their feelings down and bottle them up. And then we wonder why men are less likely to seek therapy or counseling, while being far more likely to engage in domestic violence or to use violence in general to communicate their festering emotions. If you don't give boys permission to explore their feelings, you're confining them to an emotional prison where they'll lack the emotional intelligence and general wherewithal to safely and successfully navigate those feelings later in life.

So many "weaknesses" we associate with girls are really anything but. Physical strength is often associated with men, but a 2019 study from McGill University found that women have a higher pain threshold than men.[25] Also, after being in the delivery room to watch three kids come into this world, I'll never again doubt the toughness of women. So when we tell boys to

---

25 McGill University, "Men and Women Remember Pain Differently: Strength of Finding Confirmed By Replication of Results in Mice and Men," ScienceDaily, January 10, 2019, https://www.sciencedaily.com/releases/2019/01/190110141806.htm

"man up," I'm not even sure what the hell that means; all I know is it sends a shitty and erroneous message to boys and girls that strength is somehow inherent to maleness. Also, there are many different types of strengths. Do you know how to express yourself by crying, being compassionate, and showing vulnerability? Those. Are. Not. Weaknesses. Being complete human beings who possess the capacity to feel and process emotions is an essential strength that shouldn't be gender specific in any way.

When you consider our language and how we talk about men and women, is it any wonder we have so many of the social problems we have? For hundreds of years, we've been using language that denigrates women and casts them as weak, so it should come as no surprise that women are paid less for doing the same work, are statistically likelier to be the victims of domestic abuse, are largely absent as CEOs in businesses, and are underrepresented in politics. Instead of simply telling our boys they need to be better and encouraging them to improve, we're telling them they need to be better *than girls* and to rise above the "limitations" of being a woman. It creates the foundation for misogyny and inequality, and simultaneously tells women they are somehow less than just because of their sex.

That's all in the macro, but this exists in the micro and manifests constantly in the real world, too. When Will was six years old he fell in love with the Disney animated movie *Frozen*. Like the rest of the world, he delighted in the story and especially the soundtrack. We must've watched that movie a thousand times, and he would sing all the songs and dance around like a maniac, taking legitimate and deep joy in it. But that all ended one day at the bus stop when he was talking to a little girl about *Frozen*. The girl's father cut in and said to his daughter, "Will doesn't watch *Frozen*. That's a girl movie, and he's a boy." It didn't matter that I jumped in and corrected him right away, because the damage was done. Despite loving the movie and the music, he never watched *Frozen* again. Even worse, he started parroting that same viewpoint to his friends—singing songs about plucky sisters was now something only for girls. It didn't matter that the songs and the storylines had universal appeal and were positive messages for all children. All it took was one comment from an acquaintance, and Will was put right back in the Boy Box where society thinks he belongs.

Something similar happened with Sam right as the 2016 election was heating up. While I'm an atheist, my mom is very involved with the Protestant church, and I took the kids to the church fair to support her. During their silent raffle to raise money, I bought a bunch of tickets and let the kids bid on the prize packages they wanted most. For Sam, it was a beautiful purse. Sam had always loved purses—he used them to carry his toys around, and also so he could emulate his mother. In fact, the brighter the color, the better. So, it came as absolutely no surprise when he made a beeline for the purple purse and began dumping all of his tickets toward it in the hopes of taking it home.

That's when I saw a man in his late fifties or early sixties quickly walk over to issue Sam a stern warning: "No son, not that one. That's for a purse, it's for girls—" Before he was even done speaking, I stepped in and told that man in no uncertain terms that he was never to correct my son like that, that Sam knew what he was doing, and that purses are not just for women. The man looked genuinely surprised and said he was just trying to point out the obvious, to which I responded that he was obviously behind the times. Thankfully, Sam was only three and he didn't quite register this encounter; his love of purses remains to this day. But this incident demonstrated yet another example of how men are so threatened when they perceive their masculine norms are openly "under attack" that they have no qualms instructing a stranger's son to conform to their own unhealthy ideas of what a man should and shouldn't do.

The things we say and how we say them matter more than you can possibly know. Our neighbor, with one sexist comment, sent a clear and resounding message that boys who take part in things they perceived as "feminine" and only for girls is something negative to be avoided. Nothing can be further from the truth, and our boys need to know that. (Plus, who ever decided definitively that *Frozen* and purses belong to the "feminine" realm? As we know, what is perceived as "feminine" and "masculine" come from artificial social conventions.) In order for our boys *and* girls to learn this lesson, we parents have to do better at not perpetuating messages of division and inequality that have plagued us for far too long.

PARENTING TIP #18: Eliminate "boys will be boys" and "man up" from your vocabulary

A young boy hits a girl or makes fun of her repeatedly until she cries. A teenage boy makes repeated sexual comments to a classmate, which makes her uncomfortable. A grown man running for the country's highest elected office says rich men can do whatever they want to women, including grabbing them "by the pussy." What might these three things have in common? They're all usually followed by people defending such behaviors under the rationale of "Well, boys will be boys" or claiming that it's just harmless "locker room talk." And if you're a man who dares get upset by these things and object to them publicly, you're told that you're being whiny and you need to "man up."

I've used these phrases before. I was wrong. These horrid sentiments excuse a whole host of problematic male behaviors that need to be directly addressed and rectified, not summarily dismissed and further normalized. And while I know what I'm about to describe is going to have some of you rolling your eyes, just know that these seemingly small problems with young kids that go unaddressed will grow to become bigger problems with bigger kids. While I don't have the experience of raising a little girl, I have a ton of experience watching kids interact on the playground and during play dates, and I've witnessed the following incident play out a thousand times with only slightly different variations.

Picture a group of kids around the ages of three to six all congregating in a play space. There's some climbing equipment, one of those plastic cars, and a whole bunch of LEGO, Duplo, or other blocks for kids to build. I've watched girls on the playground cede space to the rampaging hordes of boys on slides and climbing structures, in favor of wandering over to a quieter place to diligently and meticulously build things. I'd be in awe of the meticulous crafting and concentration of towers and castles constructed with great attention to detail and a laser focus—right up until some out-of-control boy came over and knocked it down with glee. This is usually met with shock at first—and then, she'd just silently build it back up again, only to have Captain Chaos come back and knock it down. Again. And again. The parents of the girl usually come in with some suggestions for their daughter, such as advising her to talk to the boy to let him know it upsets her when he knocks her tower over, or asking him to please not engage in that behavior. Here you have girls finding their own space being repeatedly invaded and their work vandalized, despite having made it clear to the aggressor that they do not wish for it to happen. They even take evasive action by moving, only to be disturbed again. Then, they watch as trusted adults come in and repeatedly let boys off the hook even though they're in the wrong, simply for the reason that they're a boy. It makes me angry. Whenever both parents eventually got together to discuss, I noticed that the boy's parents would either ignore their child's behavior or, even worse, excuse it.

"Hahaha, he's such a *boy*, right?"

"Well, that's boys being boys."

"They're just naturally so much more destructive than girls, right?"

"Oooooh, looks like my boy has a crush on your girl!"

Fuck. That. The onus continues to be on girls to calmly resolve the situation and be accommodating, while few people put the right emphasis onto curbing and preventing the problematic behavior from boys. And the boys' parents work up more of a sweat coming up with bullshit excuses for their sons instead of stepping in, letting their boys know it's not OK to ignore boundaries, and removing the boys if they don't listen in order to reinforce the idea of consequences. Believe me, I know it's a pain—Sam, my middle child, is unadulterated chaos complete with a scorching case of ADHD and Oppositional Defiant Disorder. I've had to remove Sam from many a playground because he refused to be respectful of the wishes of others. That sucks and it's difficult, but it's also necessary because I understand that excusing his behavior, even at this young age, is part of a much bigger problem that will be exacerbated with age and inattention. Look, I'm not saying a five-year-old boy is going to automatically transform from playground bully to sexual harasser, but what I am saying is that the mindset, if left unchecked, will evolve into one that has the *potential* of turning the boy into a harasser.

Using the phrase "boys will be boys" shows that you acknowledge whenever boys engage in problematic behavior, and you still excuse that behavior simply because society looks at men as innately destructive and unable to control their urges. In fact, the truth is that phrase is literally meaningless, and it does boys a disservice. Boys are not some homogenous group, and nothing is inherently written into their biological code that makes them insensitive brutes incapable of respecting boundaries and the consent of others. When we, as parents, enforce those stereotypes, it means boys will feel justified in *continuing* to act that way; and when we tell them to "man up," it sends a message to tell boys to *start* acting that way. So, stop it, and realize that your boys have the capability to be better people.

And please, for the love of all things holy, do not insinuate that parents of girls should be flattered when boys pick on their daughters because that means she's the object of his affection. If a boy is hitting a girl or picking on her until she cries, it's a sign the boy has not yet learned healthy coping mechanisms and positive ways to express his emotions—possibly because his parents or guardians haven't modeled that in their own behaviors. It is also the beginning of the road for "I hit you because I love you." That shit needs to stop early, and it'll only stop when parents of boys intervene. It's up to us to put in the work, because it's a hell of a lot easier to raise good boys than to try to change bad men.

PARENTING TIP #19: Let boys know platonic touch is OK

Boys and touching. Just reading it gives you the creeps, right? It feels dirty and wrong, probably because so much of what we hear in the news and immediately conjure up in our minds on this topic is sexual and even criminal in nature.

Let's conduct a little experiment. Picture an elementary-school-aged girl on a playground who falls off the monkey bars and hurts herself. She's crying because she's in pain, and, for whatever reason, her parents aren't right there. One of her friends, a girl, comes over. She puts her arm around her injured friend and softly whispers that it'll be OK. Or, another mom on the playground who doesn't even know the girl comes over to comfort her with a hug and some reassuring touches. That's a fine image, right? No cringing, no inappropriateness, no worries about stranger danger. Just an injured girl being comforted by other girls and women. Totally acceptable.

Now, picture the same scenario, except the injured party is a boy. Another boy is hugging him and wiping away his tears. The unaffiliated parent coming to the boy's aid is a dad. I'm willing to bet that a majority of society would have multiple problems with this scene.

First of all, boys aren't supposed to cry. The fact that he's hurt himself and is openly displaying an emotion suggests that he's weak and needs to toughen up. Second, while it is perfectly innocent for another boy to comfort his friend with a reassuring touch, I know many dads would not stand for such a thing. The ones with at least a little bit of tact might mention something about keeping their hands to themselves, while others would have no qualms about loudly telling his son that it's wrong to touch another boy. And if another man came over to hug the injured boy, that could easily end with the police being called. Dads often have to worry about being perceived as kidnappers or sexual deviants when they're caring for their own kids in public, forget hugging a stranger's kid on a playground.

Why do these perceptions occur? Well, there are a lot of reasons and a ton of issues to unpack when it comes to men and touch.

Mark Greene explored the topic beautifully and honestly in his 2018 piece "The Lack of Platonic Touch in Men's Lives is a Killer," noting that touch becomes synonymous with sex at a very early age for men. So, instead of risking an unwanted sexual touch, many men simply choose to skip touching altogether (except for the kind that comes in a romantic relationship)—a kneejerk reaction that ultimately results in men feeling isolated and confused. Greene writes: "And where does this leave men? Physically and emotionally isolated. Cut off from the human physical contact that is proven to reduce stress, encourage self-esteem and create community. Instead, we walk in the vast crowds of our cities alone in a desert of disconnection. Starving for physical connection. We crave touch. We are cut off from it. The result is *touch isolation*."[26]

While Greene is certainly not wrong, I'm happy to say this was not my experience or my upbringing. My father was raised by a good but emotionally distant man who never displayed much emotion. My grandfather had come straight off the boat from Portugal and did things how they did it in "the old country." He was solemn and silent, and displays of emotion and affection were things he believed men did not trifle with. I still remember being six and having my grandfather attempt to shake my hand as I ran up to give him a hug. Luckily, my dad was the exception who swore he'd do things differently once he became a father. He broke the cycle and passed down a healthy appreciation for platonic touch to me and my brother. To this day, even though I'm forty years old, my father gives me a hug and a kiss every single time he says hello and goodbye. During sleepovers with my guy

---

26 Mark Greene, "The Lack of Platonic Touch in Men's Lives is a Killer," *The Good Men Project*, June 1, 2018, https://goodmenproject.com/featured-content/megasahd-the-lack-of-gentle-platonic-touch-in-mens-lives-is-a-killer/

friends as preteens, we thought nothing of sleeping in the same bed because there was plenty of room—so why not?

Now, I'm the father of three boys, and we are an extremely cuddly family. I hug and kiss my boys each day when I leave for work, and then again when I get home. If we're on the couch watching TV, I think nothing of snuggling up with them. Sam, my middle child, is always game for a foot rub, which I'm happy to oblige—it makes him happy, and it never fails to make me feel closer to my boys. These habits are a natural continuation of what we used to do when they were babies—I never put them down (except to sleep), wore them around in a sling, and played with them constantly in ways that involved plenty of platonic touch. And yes, I've had people wince and cringe and even ask if I think giving my boys a kiss on the lips is a good idea, to which I perpetually reply with a resounding yes.

Six-time Super Bowl champion, New England Patriots quarterback, and GOAT (Greatest of All Time), Tom Brady, knows this particular sting of criticism. In a docuseries called *Tom vs Time* that premiered on Facebook in 2018, he kissed his oldest son on the lips, and the internet went crazy. Commenters said it was weird, creepy, and inappropriate for a father to kiss his son on the lips, all because men have been erroneously conditioned to believe that the act of kissing, especially on the lips, is solely sexual.[27] Same goes for Patriots coach and fellow GOAT, Bill Belichick, who was hit with similar attacks after celebrating one of his (many) Super Bowl wins by giving his daughter a kiss on

---

27 Gabriella Paiella, "How Do We All Feel About Tom Brady Kissing His Son on the Mouth For Like 5 Seconds at a Time," *The Cut*, February 1, 2018, https://www.thecut.com/2018/02/tom-brady-kisses-son-super-bowl-2018.html

the lips.[28] Here are two loving dads showing platonic affection to their offspring in public, and people everywhere just couldn't fathom it because men are seen as predators and that kind of affection is typically reserved for the female species. (By the way, if you think I wrote that last paragraph just to gush about the best quarterback to ever play the game for the greatest coach who ever lived on the most spectacular team in all of sports, you're absolutely correct. Deal with it, haters.)

My larger point is that when we cast men as monsters who can't control themselves, or when we perceive of them as being soft if they demonstrate physical affection, it creates an environment that causes men to actively forego platonic human contact. That kind of isolation mixed with shame isn't good for anyone. When men see each other, we generally either give each other a firm, cursory handshake; or we do that one-handed handshake-leading-into-a-hug thing where we pat each other on the back two times and immediately release so we can look away and not acknowledge the homophobia and shame that builds a wall between us. If men are sitting on a couch together, there can be absolutely no touching—either purposeful or inadvertent—and God help us all if we both reach into the chip bowl at the same time and accidentally touch fingers. It's where the problematic phrase "no homo" came from, because men don't have permission to be close or be in physical contact of a nonromantic nature without officially and for the record announcing to the world that we're bros, but definitely not gay. There's even an unwritten rule in public bathrooms that you have to leave a "gay space" while pissing at the urinal, for God's sake. Not that platonic touching

---

28 "Bill Belichick's Kiss With Daughter Causes Many to Ask: How Old is Too Old," *TODAY Show*, February 3, 2015, https://www.today.com/news/bill-belichicks-kiss-adult-daughter-raises-questions-t271

while urinating is something to be encouraged by any stretch, but it just goes to show you the lengths men go to to avoid touch, or even coming close to touch.

The truth is, scientific studies shows tangible benefits to human touch. From Tiffany Field's research showing how massage boosts the health of preterm infants[29] to Swedish researchers Asta Cekaite and Malva Kvist Holm's 2017 study that shows the soothing effect embraces have on children,[30] there are proven health benefits involved with platonic touch that help people remain happier, healthier, and more productive.

So, faced with a lack of human contact in almost all nonsexual situations, where do men get their fix of touching? For heterosexual men, the answer is from women, with whom they've entered into a sexual relationship. But, as Greene points out in his essay, this arrangement is problematic for a host of reasons. First of all, there are more men than you think who are awkward on dates not necessarily because they're shy, but because they've never known touch and literally don't know how to do it. "Hugs with men or women are a ballet of the awkward, a comedic choreography in which we turn our groins this way or that. Shoulders in, butts out, seeking to broadcast to anyone within line of sight that we are most certainly not having a sexual moment," Greene writes. At the outset of a romantic relationship, men at that point fall into one of two extremes. Either they're so neurotic about worrying their every act of affection is too overt or sexual that they fail

29 Tiffany Field, et al. "Preterm infant massage therapy research: a review." *Infant behavior & development* vol. 33,2 (2010): 115-24. doi:10.1016/j.infbeh.2009.12.004

30 Asta Cekaite and Malva Kvist Holm, "The Comforting Touch: Tactile Intimacy and Talk in Managing Children's Distress", Research on Language and Social Interaction vol. 50 (2017): 109-127. doi.org/10.1080/08 351813.2017.1301293

to take any kind of pleasure in the actual human interaction, or they are so overwhelmed by having someone to physically engage with that they completely overdo it. In the latter example, is the relationship becomes literally the only bridge to physical intimacy these men have, and so they treat it like a drug. Suddenly, their significant other is the sole gatekeeper for the entirety of their physical human interactions, which places an enormous burden on the partner to regulate things and keep them in a healthy place. Being dependent on one person for everything is generally not a healthy endeavor, which means boys are left with very few options. This is part of the reason why having a girlfriend feels like such a life-and-death situation for so many straight boys growing up. They feel like they're on a desert island with zero human physical interaction, and the only way off is to find a girl who will quench that thirst, making sexual relationships an extraordinarily high stakes endeavor fraught with fear, confusion, and desperation.

Meanwhile, when they are growing up, the main way in which boys experience nonsexual touch is via aggression—tackling on the football field, wrestling (which often happens within the context of bullying), and horseplay become the only times they are able to physically interact with other people. As boys get older, their parents often stop the cuddling and platonic touch in fear of making them "soft," and that, combined with many young men withdrawing from the dating world due to anxiety, has, at its most extreme, contributed to the creation of groups like "incels" (involuntary celibacy)—men who are looking for affection solely from women and who get angry, and even violent, when they can't get it.

Because aggressive physical contact is all they know (and is what is encouraged), boys run the risk of becoming bullies, and even when they do finally get a girlfriend, they may carry that aggression into the relationship because it's their only vocabulary. And we still wonder why so many men are the main perpetrators in cases of domestic violence, and why many others are so prone to ignoring boundaries. It's because the gentle, platonic touch they should be receiving throughout their lives stops in boyhood (if it even existed up until then) and is replaced by fear, shame, and aggression. If we gave men more outlets for positive, platonic touch, I truly believe we'd see a generation of men with a higher emotional intelligence who are far less reliant upon women and sex to fill that void.

The #MeToo movement has been an overwhelmingly positive development over the past few years. It's beyond time for people to listen to the experiences of women (and some men) and take them seriously. There is no doubt that men are the aggressors the majority of the time, and that those responsible for sexual assault and misconduct need to be named, shamed, and rooted out from their powerful perches. Unfortunately, there's another side to that coin. I've noticed the pendulum swinging too far in the other direction, when well-meaning men think an appropriate response to supporting their sisters in the movement is to spend all their time proving they're the "good guy" and not one of the "bad guys"—and, as a result, they forego any and all physical contact with women. Some are taking it to an even more troubling extreme, such as refusing to even be alone with a woman for fear of being accused of some kind of impropriety. Vice President Mike Pence, for instance, refuses to be alone with any woman who is not his wife, a fact that is troubling, considering he may have to meet with female members of his administration or a female journalist on a one-on-one basis.[31] This solution of

---

31 Gillian Tan, Katia Porzecanski, "Wall Street Rule for the #MeToo Era: Avoid Women At All Cost," *Bloomberg*, December 3, 2018, https://www.bloomberg.com/news/articles/2018-12-03/a-wall-street-rule-for-the-me-too-era-avoid-women-at-all-cost

cutting off all one-to-one interactions with women in the workplace, set by male executives who are wary of #MeToo, not only doesn't address the actual problem at hand; it also severely limits potential mentorship opportunities and the chances for women to move up the corporate ladder. What these men may not have realized is that they have shifted the spotlight from where it should be—on amplifying and listening to survivor's voices—and back onto themselves when they approach the issue with: "How can I make sure *I'm* not caught doing something wrong?" I have some wonderful female friends, and I can't imagine seeing them and not giving them a customary platonic hug, or even a kiss on the cheek. The answer to this problem is not segregation and cutting ourselves off from women; it's more communication to better understand the problem and gain insights that will help us all work together more effectively, and it's as simple as just having a fundamental respect for women as our equals.

And that's why it's up to us, this current crop of parents, to change how our young, impressionable boys view and experience life in our constantly shifting society—and it's as simple as encouraging platonic touch. As a father, that means holding my kids as much as possible, right from birth. I will continue to hug and kiss my kids (assuming they're comfortable with it) for the rest of my life. I'm going to snuggle with my boys on the couch and put my arms around them every chance I get. With my oldest on the verge of dating, I don't want him to feel shame or confusion when it comes to platonically touching someone versus initiating a sexual touch. I also want to make sure he's not restricted by homophobia when it comes to offering his male friends a hug or a shoulder squeeze if someone is going through a rough time or just because someone needs some nonsexual human connection.

At the root of our entire experience is human connection, and it is insane to think that we are preventing our boys from experiencing and being clear about something so basic. We all need to touch and be touched in ways that have nothing to do with sex, and as parents, we must ensure we're not robbing our kids of vital human interaction.

PARENTING TIP #20: It's OK for boys to feel sad and seek help

It took me years to muster up the courage to walk into a therapist's office because I was afraid of being perceived as weak. I was convinced that men don't need to complain about or share their problems, and by the time I finally did go, I had been struggling with minor depression for years. When I think of all the lost time, delayed progress, and literal years spent not being the best version of myself for my family, I feel deep shame. Unfortunately, the shame society bestows on men who talk about their feelings or who seek outside help in sorting out their emotions is deeper and profoundly more frightening. And I'm far from alone.

According to Mental Health America, more than six million men experience depressive tendencies every single year, much of which goes undiagnosed.[32] The American Psychological Association says 9 percent of men have daily feelings of depression or anxiety, and nearly one-third of all men suffer from a prolonged period of depression over the course of their lifetime. But the most alarming statistic everyone needs to know and too few people are talking about is that the suicide rate among American men is about four times higher than that among

---

32 "Infographic: Mental Health for Men," *Mental Health America*, https://www.mhanational.org/infographic-mental-health-men

women. The number is especially high among elderly white men.[33]

Clearly, men are in crisis. So, why don't more of these men seek assistance? Well, it's because "only pussies ask for help, you little bitch."

The prevailing thought among a majority of men (and far too many women, frankly) is that men should handle their problems themselves—and if they can't deal with it on their own, then they're not really men. Oh, and by the way, "dealing with it" in the realm of stereotypical masculinity does not mean baring your soul to a counselor or therapist to work on the root causes of the distress, since getting all up in our feelings is something we believe only women do. Instead, men are taught to deal with their shit in a variety of unhelpful ways that not only fail to help the men who need it but also simultaneously harm society.

Ever seen the movie *Fight Club*? The reason it's beloved by hordes of men is because it gives men validation that our problems can be solved through enhanced aggression. Hell, the first fucking rule about Fight Club is not to talk, and the rest of the movie tries to convince men that they will feel a whole lot better about their problems if they just beat the shit out of each other. Basically, how are we taught to deal with our problems? Unleash all that aggression in the form of violence. Solid plan, right?

Besides violence, what other options do men have? Alcohol and drug use, for example, are apparently perfectly acceptable ways to cope with a problem. Who doesn't love a hard-drinking, strong, silent type who takes his counsel from Drs. Daniels, Walker, and Beam instead of, you know, an actual doctor? According to statistics from the Centers for Disease Control and Prevention, men

---

33 "By the Numbers: Men and Depression," *American Psychological Association* 46, no. 11 (December 2015): 13.

are nearly two times more likely to binge drink than women, with 23 percent of men reporting they had binged on alcohol at least five times in the last month, averaging eight drinks per binge. The CDC also found that men have consistently higher rates of alcohol-related deaths and hospitalizations than women, are twice as likely to have been legally intoxicated in a fatal car crash as women, and are more likely compared to women to have engaged in drinking prior to committing suicide.[34]

And if aggression and substance abuse can't solve what's ailing us, then it's time for the old standby, which is "shut up and man up." That's where I landed for so many years, causing myself and my family unnecessary pain and anguish while I pretended nothing was wrong, all in the name of ignorant emotional stoicism and holding on to a fictional "Man Card" steeped in bullshit and outdated tropes about manhood.

Guys, let me tell you something right now: asking for help when you need it is not a weakness. It's not soft, and it doesn't make you less of a man. In fact, making sure you get the help you need so you can be the best husband and father possible is the height of masculinity. It is indicative of strength and a desire to be a better person, and it doesn't matter that you needed help to get there. We all need help sooner or later. We're a society made up of communities held together by personal relationships and strengthened by a desire for human aid and connection. We all are helped and we all help others, so men need to get over this antiquated bullshit of thinking there's inherent value in walling ourselves off emotionally, only to hasten our spiritual and emotional decline. Now, when my male friends and I get together for

---

34 "Fact Sheets – Excessive Alcohol Use and Risks to Men's Health," Centers for Disease Control and Prevention, accessed September 15, 2019, https://www.cdc.gov/alcohol/fact-sheets/mens-health.htm

beers around the fire or our fantasy football draft, we're not just there to get loaded and debate whether Tom Brady is the GOAT compared to Joe Montana (he is, by the way). We also open up about the difficulties we're facing in our lives, such as marriage troubles, dissatisfaction with work-life balance, and feelings of inadequacy as fathers and men. We also celebrate milestones and take joy in the direction our lives have taken. The point is, we talk about our deeper issues, and we feel supported by our community, not condemned. Each of us have been turned upside-down on a spinning Wheel of Fortune, and we know that none of us have turned our fate back around on a solo basis.

More men need to understand that strength and silence are not natural companions, and that it's OK to talk things through. I'm not exaggerating when I say a failure to realize this, and succumbing to toxic masculinity where our mental health is concerned, is literally killing us. But there's actually no earthly reason for it to be this way. Women have networks and friendships that can be relied upon when the chips are down, and men are not biologically prevented from doing the same. We need to be alive, first. We need to be less angry. We need to be healthier and to communicate more. If more men took that to heart, I believe with every fiber of my being that we'd see a better, healthier, less deadly version of men.

Part of solving this problem is not being afraid, as parents, to show our kids we're vulnerable. It's OK to tell our kids we're sad and talk about the reasons why (in an age-appropriate way). Some will say that's putting our problems on our kids, but I think it's vital for our children to know we struggle, too, and to also let them see us actively fixing the problem. If kids see us model the behavior of asking for help when necessary and talking about our problems, they'll be more likely to do the same when problems of their own arise, and you'll open up a vital channel for honest communication in your family.

PARENTING TIP #21: Let boys pursue nontraditional interests

When I envisioned myself as the father of a strapping young lad, I had certain things in mind for him. At the top of list? A deep and unrelenting love of sports. I played three sports a year growing up and went to baseball and basketball camp. We've also had season tickets to the New England Patriots my entire life, so I've gone to hundreds of football games. I put the fan in fanatic, and then some, and I assumed that because I loved something so much, my kids would just naturally fall into that, too.

So, imagine my surprise when my oldest son came home one day when he was in the second grade and said, "Dad, I'm taking a scrapbooking class!"

Even at the age of seven, my son hated baseball. It was too slow for him, and he flat out had no interest in it. He's always been very tall for his age, so I thought basketball would be an option, but no dice there. He's slow as molasses, having inherited his mother's (lack of) grace and coordination. Hockey would've been a giraffe-on-ice disaster of epic proportions, and there was no way I was going to let him play football with all the CTE research that's come out. So, team sports, which served as the bedrock of my childhood and gave me some of my fondest memories, were completely out with him from a pretty early age.

In their place are things I never could have imagined. While I went to basketball camp at Massachusetts Maritime Academy and College of the Holy Cross, do you know what Will did that summer? He attended Farm-to-Table camp—an entire week of learning how to cook, visiting local farms, and mulling over recipes using fresh food they picked themselves. And oh, how he loves to cook. Donning his pink apron, he's obsessed with ingredients and entranced by how everything comes together to make a meal. Will had another elective he could choose that year, and at first, to my surprise, he chose football. My kid, the gentlest of giants and most gloriously uncoordinated kid on the planet, chose football. I didn't need to ask him why—he had done it to make me happy. It was a gesture I thanked him for and then immediately balked at because I knew his heart wasn't in it. Know what he really wanted to do? Take a class on Rainbow Loom—a plastic tool used to weave colorful rubber and plastic bands into decorative items such as bracelets and charms. It's absolutely true to who Will is, and that's just fine by me. I would never want to change my kids to make them more like me; it's not responsible parenting, and I have no interest in bringing up a clone.

Back to scrapbooking. He knew that he'd be the only boy in the class and that he was violating society's unwritten rules about what was meant for boys and girls, but he did it anyway. On the first day, his well-meaning teacher drove home the boy-girl binary by pushing red or blue material instead of the pink, yellow, and purple he had picked out on his own. Will calmly told her he was happy with his colors and also reminded her that there are no actual "boy" or "girl" colors. He quietly went about his business, comfortable with himself and the fact that he was doing something he truly enjoyed. I wish I had the strength and self-confidence now, at age forty, that my son had at seven! But while I was never strong enough as a kid to do the things I liked for myself, I'm now making up for it by raising a self-assured and confident young man who does what feels right to him no matter the response. It sounds simple, but it's actually an amazing and rare thing. And it shouldn't be, because all kids should be able to do what makes them happy. Unfortunately, that's just not the reality for far too many boys.

Our kids won't always follow in our footsteps, but we can lead them down a better path than the one we had walked on when we were younger. One of the most important ways we can do that is to remain open and to let them try new and unexpected things. Things that may make you cringe. Things you'd be embarrassed to tell your friends. Things that leave you feeling unsure and uncomfortable. The older I get, the more I realize that being uncertain is not such a bad place to be. It means my worldview is being challenged, that I'm being forced to think deeply about why I'm upset or uncomfortable. They don't always tell you that parenting means learning just as much from our kids as they do from us, but it's the truth.

Never was that truth more apparent than in 2018 when Sam was bullied for painting his fingernails. Ten years ago, I don't think I would've let him—at least, I wouldn't have let him go out the door; I'd have been standing by with the polish remover out and ready. And I would've convinced myself that I was doing it for him, but that would've been a lie. It would've been for my own comfort and benefit, so I wouldn't have to feel uncomfortable or ashamed by the condescension from relatives and friends.

The truly sad part is I would've ignored the golden rule of parenting: which is love and support your kids no matter what. I also would have missed out on all the wonderful aspects of Sam's personality, if I had spent all my time trying to hide it away. It's unimaginable to me, now, to think of dulling the light that is my middle child's personality, including muffling his bright, beautiful nails. Does participating in a traditionally feminine activity like painting nails throw up a few added obstacles for boys like

Sam? Yes. But so fucking what? We navigate those like we have to navigate all the other crap that inevitably and invariably arise as we grow up. It would have been much worse for Sam to have to navigate the emotional trauma of his father being ashamed of him for something so simple as brightly colored nail polish. Worse, Sam would have had to give in the fight to toxic masculinity. I'm forever thankful I woke the hell up and removed my head from my ass before it was too late.

It's our job as parents to give kids the latitude and judgment-free space to try new things in order to become more complete human beings. And you just might get a lot more locally sourced organic dinners, gorgeous scrapbooks, beautiful elastic band bracelets, and maybe even viral Twitter fame from an on-point fingernail polish game.

PARENTING TIP #22: Avoid harmful double standards for boys and girls (especially when it comes to dating)

Most parents treat boys and girls differently. It starts with finding out you're expecting and wondering if you're going to have a ball player or a ballerina, and it goes right up until they start dating and you're high-fiving your son who has just gotten a girlfriend while simultaneously digging a moat to keep suitors away from your daughter. In between these are a million other little things that seem innocuous but that, in actuality, show our sons and daughters there are different rules for them depending on your sex. That's why, as parents, we need to be cognizant of how we treat boys versus girls and make sure we're not sending damaging messages to kids based on these arbitrary differences.

Unfortunately, these differences can manifest themselves even in the delivery room immediately after children are born. Talking to and playing with infants will improve cognitive and language skills in newborns, who are primed for communication even shortly after birth. A study by Dr. Betty Vohr at Women & Infants Hospital in Rhode Island found that mothers respond more to infant girls than boys, which could be attributed to the fact that girls are more cognitively advanced and with better language skills than boys early in life.[35] So, not only do we talk to boys and girls differently (boys get a lot of "Hey, champ" and "How ya doing, sport?" while girls get "Hello there, beautiful princess"), but we also talk significantly less to boys in general.

Then, when they get a little older and their personalities start to develop more fully, boys and girls quickly learn that assertiveness is not looked at in the same light for boys compared to girls. If a little boy clearly vocalizes what he wants, he's generally praised, and people remark about his confidence and leadership abilities. But when a girl loudly states her preferences, she's often seen as bossy and even rude. In sports, aggressiveness on the field of play is seen as mandatory for boys, while girls are generally encouraged to be more demure. Having attended many youth sporting events for my own kids, I can tell you that aggressive physical play, hogging the ball, and individual glory is praised at every turn when it comes to boys, yet girls of the same age and who play the same sport together with these boys are encouraged to pass the ball and generally have more of a focus on teamwork. And when kids get hurt playing sports, the gender divide couldn't be any more pronounced. No one bats an eyelash if a girl sheds some tears after she's been injured, but if a boy sustains

---

35 Katharine Johnson, Melinda Caskey, Katherine Rand, Richard Tucker, Betty Vohr, "Gender Differences in Adult-Infant Communication in the First Months of Life", *Pediatrics*, Nov 2014, peds.2013-4289; **DOI:** 10.1542/peds.2013-4289

the same injury, parental shouts of "It's OK, bud, walk it off" can always be heard all over the field or court.

These behaviors are so drilled into us and so much a part of our worldviews that it can be difficult to even recognize that we're treating our kids differently based on sex. But we need to try—because our kids notice. They soak all of that in, and it'll become a large part of how their outlook on these issues is formed. For example, boys begin to realize they're rewarded not necessarily for being right, but for being unquestionably confident with their actions and opinions. Parents who don't take note of these things and who don't work toward a more egalitarian line of thinking might inadvertently be telling their sons to win at all costs while ignoring real injuries and harm. Meanwhile, when their girls are punished for assertiveness, they'll learn from it and blend into the background instead.

So, have the same expectations for your kids no matter what genitalia they have. Double standards based on sex are just as harmful on the field as they are in the classroom, and if left untreated they will lead to disparities at home and ultimately in the office.

But perhaps nowhere else is this double standard so appalling and sexist as when we're talking about parental attitudes toward boys and girls when they start dating. The different rules we have for dating-age boys and girls are out of control, reflecting a genuine missed opportunity for parents to have a healthy and productive conversation with their kids about dating.

Here's an example of one such double standard, which I've briefly discussed before: when parents joke about threatening the boys who try to date their daughter. Let's get a few things out of the way first. Being apprehensive and concerned when your kids reach dating age is something to which just about every parent can relate, and wanting to protect your kids at all costs is a perfectly normal wish. And yes, wanting your kids to date someone with a solid character and upbringing is also totally understandable. But as with everything else in life, being aware of the different rules you may unwittingly be setting for boys and girls is key.

Let me put it bluntly: if you're a parent who openly threatens, scares, and intimidates boys who have a crush on your "little princess," or if you use guns as a prop to threaten, scare, and intimidate said boys, you're being an asshole. Unfortunately, the parenting and media landscape is filled with messaging that normalizes this idiocy and even makes it seem like it's good parenting to threaten a minor with physical violence.

One of the clips that never fails to make the rounds on social media when the topic of kids dating arises is from the 2003 movie *Bad Boys 2*, starring Martin Lawrence and Will Smith. Known as "The Reggie Scene," it involves a fifteen-year-old boy knocking on the door to Lawrence's house and politely asking to take his daughter out on a first date. In the two minutes that follow, Lawrence and Smith swear at him, search him without cause, threaten him with physical harm, force him to disclose whether he's sexually active, wave a gun in his face, and then Will Smith's character threatens him with prison rape. Two grown men—who work as police officers, by the way, with the duty to protect and serve the public—hold a fifteen year old at gunpoint and threaten to sodomize him and end his life, simply because he respectfully asked to go on one date with Lawrence's daughter. The scene is widely held as the gold standard and go-to for people (mostly men) if they wish to discuss on social media how to handle their daughters' would-be male suitors.

And that's just a movie. There are plenty of real-life examples of this bullshit. Former NFL player turned CBS commentator, Jay Feely, tweeted a picture of himself in 2018 standing between his teenage daughter and his daughter's boyfriend, with one hand on her shoulder and the other holding a gun.[36] And in 2014, retired US Navy Seal Marcus Luttrell's Facebook post went viral for describing the grueling prerequisites his daughter's future boyfriends would have to meet in order to date her, as well as referring to himself as a "maniac" chained to the wall with a bad temper to deter boyfriends.[37]

And then there are the various online groups referring to themselves as DADD, which stands for *Dads Against Daughters Dating*. It's not as dumb, juvenile, and short-sighted as it sounds; it's much worse. You can spot these guys by the T-shirts they like to wear so much, which all have slightly different messages but run along the same theme of "I'm armed, I'm creepily gatekeeping my daughter's virginity, and I will fuck up any boy who comes round these parts because I'm a grown man who takes a weird amount of pride in being able to beat up minors." An actual version of one such shirt reads "Dads Against Daughters Dating: Shoot the First One and the Word Will Spread," while another literary gem says "Rules for Dating My Daughter: 1. Get a job; 2. Understand I don't like you; 3. I am everywhere; 4. You hurt her, I hurt you; 5. Be home 30 minutes early; 6. Get a lawyer; 7. If you lie to me I will find out; 8. She is my princess, not

---

36 Cindy Boren, "CBS Announcer Jay Feely Says Posing With a Gun in Daughter's Prom Photo was 'A Joke'," *Washington Post*, April 22, 2018, https://www.washingtonpost.com/news/early-lead/wp/2018/04/22/cbs-announcer-jay-feely-says-posing-with-a-gun-in-daughters-prom-photo-was-a-joke/

37 Caroline Bologna, "Navy SEAL's Intimidating Rules for Dating His Daughter Go Viral," *Huffington Post*, October 6, 2014, https://www.huffpost.com/entry/navy-seal-rules-for-raising-daughter_n_5940088

your conquest; 9. I don't mind going back to jail; 10. Whatever you do to her, I will do to you."[38]

I can already hear some of you saying, "Calm down, it's just a joke." Except there's nothing funny about it. There are a number of terrible messages hidden in this way of thinking, and these godawful tropes need to die the quickest of deaths. First, what kind of a man threatens a child with a gun? Guns aren't ever a joke, even if it's used as a prop. Second, check out a common defense from fathers who engage in this asinine behavior: "Well, I remember what I was like at that age, so I'm not taking any chances." For starters, here is actually a perfect situation to claim the often misused #NotAllMen. Not all men will engage in reprehensible behaviors with their date that will earn them such threats of violence from fathers. I'm raising three boys who have great manners and respect for other people, and while they will definitely be subject to the whims of raging hormones, I know I've raised them to not act on their impulses at the expense of others. The other point is, it's also incredibly ironic that these fathers would use, as an excuse for their ridiculous behavior, the example of how *they'd* acted wrongfully toward women in the past. If overprotective fathers threatening them with guns and physical violence didn't intimidate them into behaving appropriately in the past, why do they think their actions are going to deter would-be male suitors now? It's time to try something new—genuine conversations with boys that set expectations, while simultaneously teaching girls how to make their own healthy dating choices.

Third, this attitude of the overprotective dad does our daughters a tremendous disservice. When well-meaning but egregiously off-base dads clamor to protect their daughters from their dates,

---

38 Silk Road Tees, "Rules for dating my daughter Men's T-shirt gift for Best Dad Father's Day T-shirt," *Amazon.com,* https://www.amazon.com/Silk-Road-Tees-Daughter-T-Shirt/dp/B079NPLKY7

they reveal that they are thinking of their daughters as property and that they are treating them like porcelain dolls. Contrary to the dangerous stereotype, girls are not mindless objects that need to be protected so their virginity—and, subsequently, their value as human beings—remains unblemished. To equate a girl's virginity with her inherent worth shows just how much society has failed our girls. This was never more clear than in November 2019 when rapper TI told the world he takes his eighteen-year-old daughter to the gynecologist on an annual basis specifically to make sure her hymen is still intact.[39] Putting aside the fact that the hymen can be broken as a result of other activities, the World Health Organization has called such practices medically unnecessary and also "painful, humiliating, and traumatic." Not to mention, just *super* creepy and inappropriate. What would TI have done if her hymen was broken? Send her back and get a replacement? Disown her? He should spend this much time and effort making sure she's prepared to make healthy choices and cementing himself as a trusted resource for her, instead of demanding doctors check on the status of her virginity.

The truly ironic part is, in my personal experience, as well as according to other men I've talked to, I've observed that girls mature much faster than boys. At eleven years old, I was corralled by a slightly older girl into a YMCA supply closet and into my first kiss, and right up to that very moment, I had had no idea that tongues were involved in kissing. The idea of girls (and women) making the first move and being assertive with their sexuality is very difficult for some people to accept. The larger point is that girls can be just as sexually curious as boys and just

---

39 Ben Beaumont-Thomas, "Outrage as US rapper TI says he has his daughter's hymen checked annually," *The Guardian*, Nov. 7, 2019, https://www.theguardian.com/music/2019/nov/07/ti-rapper-daughter-hymen-check-outrage

as experimental. The dads who imagine their little princesses as perpetual toddlers in need of protection simply have blinders on. The saddest part about maintaining such attitudes and double standards is that parents are missing a golden opportunity to talk with their daughters about dating and sex in a meaningful way, where they would be building a healthy foundation and opening a line of communication that would prove far more effective at actually safeguarding their daughters than waving a gun at boys.

The fantastic essay by Ferrett Steinmetz, "Dear Daughter: I Hope You Have Some Fucking Awesome Sex,"[40] has a title that will make just about everyone cringe; however, the crux of the piece is a loving, heart-warming, and genuine promise from a father to his daughter to support her in a way that doesn't demean or diminish her. He tells his daughter he hopes she has *fantastic* sex that is freely given on her part and revolves around giving and receiving mutual pleasure. While he has no desire to hear about the details of said sex, he tells his daughter in no uncertain terms that sex is an important human connection, and having it, as a woman, is not inherently degrading or negative. And any man who thinks it is likely isn't worth her time.

Parents need to stop assuming that all girls are innocent bystanders in their love lives while boys are perpetual predators who should be the subject of automatic parental vitriol. When we plaster that mindset onto T-shirts, commemorate it in summer blockbusters, and proudly pass it around social media circles, we're telling boys that they're the inherent villains and that girls are their helpless prey. It tells our girls that they lack agency and that the ability to make decisions regarding their own bodies belongs to their fathers. Also, imagine if a parent were to threaten

---

40 Ferrett Steinmetz, "Dear Daughter: I Hope You Have Some Fucking Awesome Sex," *TheFerrett.com*, August 8, 2013, https://www.theferrett. com/2013/08/08/dear-daughter-i-hope-you-have-some-fucking-awesome-sex/

a girl attempting to date their son in the hopes of protecting their precious boy's virginity! You see just how wrong that sounds.

Parents, just don't play along with these stereotypes. If someone "jokes" about cleaning a gun if your boy comes over to date their daughter, let them know in a respectful but straightforward way that isn't funny. No one is making the case for teenagers to do whatever they want and to have irresponsible sex; I'm saying there's a better way to help kids make informed, respectful, and healthy decisions that doesn't involve threats, gatekeeping, and misogynistic, patriarchal bullshit that hurts both boys and girls. We need to have the difficult and uncomfortable conversations about sex with our kids because, when we do, they will learn they have a safe space where trust has been built and nurtured. Parents treating kids with the same set of rules and expectations regardless of sex projects egalitarianism and equality—traits worthy of emulation when *they* go on to have their own kids.

PARENTING TIP #23: Don't teach boys that sexual abuse is acceptable

When I was in eighth grade, I distinctly remember being infatuated with one of our substitute teachers. She was young, effervescent, blonde, and I thought she was the most beautiful woman I'd ever seen. A bunch of us boys would always marvel at her and wonder which of us she'd choose to be with if the opportunity ever presented itself outside of school. We were thirteen years old, dumb as rocks, and navigating a sea of raging hormones and miniscule knowledge of what was happening to our bodies.

One day, we were all hanging out at someone's house, and the subject about wanting to be romantically involved with our teacher came up again—only this time, our friend's dad was in the room. When we realized that he'd heard us, I worried we'd be in trouble. However, that wasn't the case. Instead, he kind of smiled and said, "You *wish* you were that lucky."

I thought it was funny at the time. Now? Well, I've realized our friend's dad basically told a bunch of thirteen-year-old boys that we'd be "lucky" to be raped.

There's a seminal moment in the movie *A Time to Kill* when Matthew McConaughey's character is attempting to convince a jury to acquit his client, played by Samuel L. Jackson. Jackson, a black father in racially charged Mississippi, is on trial for killing the two white men who raped and tortured his young daughter. With the all-white jury champing at the bit to convict his client, McConaughey makes them close their eyes as he painstakingly details the unspeakable horrors visited upon the young girl. But because he knows the jury is racist and unable to see her as human, the lawyer makes one final plea.

"Now, imagine she's white."

I thought of this scene when I was researching the string of incidents involving female teachers having sex with their underage students.[41] The trend seems to be similar in all the cases, with attractive teachers in their twenties and early thirties allegedly initiating sexual contact with children ranging in age from thirteen to seventeen. In some cases, the affairs last for years even though some of the teachers are married and have families. Here's where I harness my inner Matthew McConaughey:

"Now, imagine it's a male teacher—and the student is female."

When we hear about teachers who sexually abuse their students, we often imagine a creepy male teacher who has taken advantage of

---

41 Paul Larosa, "'48 Hours' Investigates Sex Abuse by Women Teachers," *CBS News*, October 17, 2014, https://www.cbsnews.com/news/48-hours-investigates-sex-abuse-by-women-teachers/

a naïve, innocent female student. We label the abuser a *sicko, pervert,* and *child molester.* Fathers talk about the beatings they would inflict on the monster who dared violate their little girl. Heads shake in unison at the horrors the young, innocent victim had had to endure at the hands of a disgusting criminal. But here are some of the things I've heard and read people say when stories about female teachers taking advantage of male students make the headlines.

"Good for him!"

"Where were those teachers when I was in school?"

"Wow. That's the luckiest kid in the world."

It's heartbreaking to think the sexual abuse of a child is some-how mitigated because the victim is a teenage boy rather than a girl. Even more insidious is the idea that these boys aren't really victims, but rather victors, in this scenario—the fathers who talk of pummeling the men who violate their girls suddenly change their tone and speak of high-fiving their sons should they ever bed a hot female teacher.

An immature teenage boy is just as likely as an immature teenage girl to be confused and ashamed if he is taken advantage of by an authority figure he's supposed to trust. It gets worse when he's then told by society that he is lucky and should actually be thankful for what happened. Imagine the horror and revulsion if we told female students that they were lucky to score a fling with a hot male teacher. These boys have been violated by an adult during their adolescence, and they will likely face serious and long-lasting repercussions down the road that will affect them for years to come. When a teacher uses the significant power differ-ential to abuse a minor sexually, no matter how "hot" the media claims they are, that is sexual abuse. And that is always unacceptable, regardless of the sex of the perpetrator and victim.

My friend's dad wasn't a bad guy by any stretch, but hearing him tell me I should thank my lucky stars if I were ever raped twisted me up pretty good. Again, having different rules for boys and girls based on the warped way we view sex and masculinity is sending a truly damaging message to kids—especially boys. Adults are supposed to protect kids, yet when boys see society approve of relationships between adult female teachers and minor boys, it perpetuates the harmful stereotype of boys as walking erections built to fuck on command. It conveys the idea that boys should seek out praise for every sexual conquest, even in scenarios in which they are the victim of a crime and an abusive relationship. These boys will then grow up to become men who look at women as a way to up their status; they'll tie their self-worth to how big they can grow their misogynistic trophy cases. And this is harmful to both women and men.

As parents, it's our responsibility to make sure we're sending the right messages to our kids, especially on the issue of sex and especially with our boys, so they understand boundaries and have healthy views on appropriate sexual conduct and their own self-worth. If boys see parents legitimately upset about male teachers abusing girls and vowing to protect their daughters at all costs, but then see those same parents *praising* the boys who are "lucky" enough to be raped, that's a devastating mixed message—one that will have negative and harmful repercussions for years to come.

Our boys, our men, and our society deserve so much better.

PARENTING TIP #24: Have a social media plan for your kids

Sooner or later, your kids will start engaging with social media. While I am on social media every day, have received numerous career opportunities because of it, and have developed extraordinarily meaningful friendships with people all over the world whom I wouldn't have met without it, I am so grateful social media wasn't prevalent during my childhood. When I think of all the stupid and insane things I did as a kid in the eighties and early nineties, and imagine those things being captured by smartphones and plastered onto YouTube, Twitter, Instagram, Facebook, and Snapchat in real time, it sends a shiver down my spine. Kind of like the cold sweat that envelopes me now that my oldest has limited access to Instagram.

For starters, the bullying that occurs on social media and gaming platforms is very real and very much a problem. While part of what makes the Internet great is its global connectedness, if your kid is getting picked on online, that connectivity will also make it feel like there's no escape. When I was growing up, at least the bullying at school mercifully stopped when the final bell rang. Now it continues after school on social media platforms and group texts—and when kids gang up on each other via headsets while playing Fortnite.

My oldest son was ten in 2018 when we let him have an Xbox and an Instagram account, and he was eleven when he received his first cellphone. In 2008, when I first became a parent, my wife and I swore he wouldn't have either of those things until he was at least a teenager. It turned out, in this growing age of connectivity, that he would be one of the last kids in his friend group to receive those items. We could have held fast to our rule, but the fact of the matter was that kids were already congregating on Xbox and communicating through Instagram Stories and Snaps. It's the "playground" of his youth and just the way kids communicate with each other these days. Will still plays outside and runs around our neighborhood with his friend, but then they'll decide to break off into their own homes to meet online and talk virtually.

We opted to ease him into the world of online video games and social media—but with trepidation and nonnegotiable rules.

We made it clear that his cell phone really isn't his—it's ours. We're allowing him to use it, and because of this understanding, we can inspect it anytime we want. There are varying schools of thought on whether parents should read their kids' texts, and I understand that some parents think it's a violation of trust to do that. There's merit to that argument. However, I have no apologies or reservations about being the parent who goes through my kid's phone on occasion—with his knowledge. Despite being a generally responsible kid, Will is still an eleven-year-old with a brain that is still developing. And while I'm all about letting my kids make mistakes from which they can learn, technology presents certain situations that can cause permanent harm stemming from a single incident.

When I was working as a journalist at the *Cape Cod Times* in 2009, I bylined a story that stopped me dead in my tracks and made me realize how problematic technology could be and how our laws weren't keeping up with the times. In February 2009, I learned that six boys, ages twelve to fourteen, were being summonsed to court in front of a clerk magistrate who would decide if they would face child pornography charges despite being minors themselves.[42] The infraction stemmed from one of the boys taking a topless picture of a thirteen-year-old female classmate, which he then forwarded to friends via text. By the letter of the law in Massachusetts, their actions potentially constituted felony charges of dissemination of child pornography. It was the first time I ever encountered the term *sexting*, and

---

42 Aaron Gouveia, "Police: Sexting Photo is Sexually Explicit," *Cape Cod Times*, February 28, 2009, https://www.capecodtimes.com/article/20090228/news/902280323?template=ampart

the whole thing turned into a national story that consisted of appearances on *Inside Edition* and in *People Magazine*. One of the fathers even turned the ordeal into a book. It was eye-opening for many parents in the area because, for the first time, it put the full extent of the potential legal ramifications that kids could face in the digital age on display. Many people were shocked that the act of an underaged kid forwarding a sexual picture of an underage girl to a friend, even if he hadn't taken the picture, could be looked at in the same light as child porn.

Unfortunately, the father who served as the spokesman for the group of boys chose to blame everyone but his son, and that's where things took a toxic turn. Despite the father's admission that what his son had done was wrong, he never instructed his son to apologize to the girl in the photo.[43] The boy was given a new phone immediately after the police confiscated his old one. They also took a father-son trip to New York City in the wake of the incident, courtesy of *Inside Edition*, which paid for their airfare, limo service, a five-star hotel, and $675 in spending money. The book *A Father's Sexting Teen: The Brian Hunt Story*,[44] which he coauthored with a writer in California, includes details of how he and his son toured Times Square, Central Park, Ellis Island, and the Statue of Liberty, and even went for a rickshaw ride during their stay. The book goes on to blame the media for blowing things out of proportion, the school for involving the police department, and the police department for being overzealous in its pursuit of charges. It even refers to the boy as a "victim." Finally, the authors

---

43 Aaron Gouveia, "Falmouth Father Details Sexting Story," *Cape Cod Times*, November 29, 2010, https://www.capecodtimes.com/article/20101129/NEWS/11290308

44 Annie Winston and Brian Hunt, "A Father's Sexting Teen: The Brian Hunt Story, *CreateSpace Independent Publishing Platform*, https://www.amazon.com/Fathers-Sexting-Teen-Brian-story/dp/1456334441, Nov. 23, 2010

blame the thirteen-year-old girl, saying: "The one who creates the picture is the one who started the problem. As far as the girl and her culpability, she posed for the picture. No one had a gun to her head." The book repeatedly calls for "purity" and the final chapters emphasize the importance of abstinence to help teens avoid "demoralizing and devaluing their God-given dignity."

So, a boy takes a picture of a partially naked girl, sends it to his friends, those male friends send it to more friends, and then the parents of the boys try to pin it on the girl, simply because she posed for it? The theme of victim blaming presents itself far too often these days, and it's absolutely a part of toxic masculinity. Unfortunately, for this one boy, I doubt he learned anything except how to blame everyone else for his problems, thanks in large part to his father.

In the decade since that incident, the prevalence of social media in our lives has increased, along with the risks for our children. That's why I check my son's phone regularly. It's why I have Google Family Link, which allows me to turn his phone on and off at will, set usage limits, and make it so the phone is useless except for emergency calls every day from 8:00 p.m. to 7:00 a.m. It's why I also have an app on his phone that constantly scans for language that denotes bullying, alcohol and drug use, and self-harming language and that notifies me immediately if it detects something is wrong. All that said, while using technology to safeguard the technology we give our kids is well and good, the real value is in the frank discussions we have with our children to give them a true basis of understanding regarding these issues. Although he was only ten, I spoke at length with Will about the case of the sexting teens, the ramifications of bullying of any kind either in real life or virtually, and the potential fallout from taking and sharing inappropriate pictures. I never sneak around to spy on him—I ask him to sit with me and we look through his phone together and talk about anything inappropriate or problematic on there. Is it awkward? Yeah, sometimes. But from there, we build trust. As long as he's showing me he understands the rules and isn't having any issues, he'll get more and more latitude.

With an easily traceable digital footprint and Google knowing just about everything we do on the internet, it's also important for parents, not just kids, to be cognizant of our social media use and how it may affect our kids in the future. This is especially tricky for parent bloggers like myself, who use material from our daily lives as the basis for our stories. When our kids are young, it seems like a non-issue since we own most of the stories—sleepless nights, diaper blowouts, teaching our toddler to walk and talk, etc. But remember that your kids will get older—they will enter school, learn to read, and eventually find the internet. I'll never forget the first time one of Will's friends left a comment on a YouTube video I'd posted from when Will was about five years old—he was tearfully asking the internet if they had seen his lost stuffed animal. It suddenly dawned on me that I was no longer telling my story; I was telling his. And his story isn't all mine to tell. So, we made some rules around my social media use, and I promised to ask each of the boys for their permission before posting anything that involved them on my channels. Most of the time they're fine with it, but sometimes they say no, and that's perfectly OK.

There is absolutely such a thing as oversharing, and I'm guilty as charged on several occasions. The important thing is that parents set boundaries for our kids and ourselves, and we do it via open and constant communication because maintaining a dialogue should always be one of our top priorities. Whether you use a monitoring program or you're planning to be a social media holdout, it's imperative you have a plan and discuss that plan with your kids. Talk about online bullying, exclusion, and responsible and respectful social media use. That includes having discussions about nudity, sexting, and graphic content, as well as any potential legal ramifications. These things aren't easy or pleasant, but they're very necessary.

Chapter 4

It's Time to Get Controversial

M Y GRANDMOTHER ALWAYS SAID, "NEVER TALK POLITICS OR religion." But she didn't live in the age of Make America Great Again, alternative facts, Twitter, the twenty-four-hour news cycle, and this batshit-crazy climate in which truth seems to matter less than blind allegiance. So, with apologies to Grandma, I'm about to get pretty controversial because it is not only impossible to avoid talking about these things in front of or with your children; it's also shortsighted and, I'd argue, irresponsible.

Racism, misogyny, bigotry, and alpha-male nonsense has always been present in American culture, so I'm not blaming Donald Trump's rise to power for the introduction of these societal ills. What I am saying, without an ounce of hesitation or equivocation, is that since Trump became president in 2016, he has legitimized and even encouraged these belief systems. Because of Trump, fellow morons feel enabled to spew their toxic bullshit in public, and it's quickly becoming the norm. He's cleared the way for white nationalists to come out of their basements and into the mainstream, made pussy-grabbing a presidential trait, turned back the clock on the LGBTQ+ movement, and single-handedly made being an egomaniacal strongman fashionable while simultaneously vilifying what we've always considered good leadership qualities—having experience, education, and a calm demeanor. It's as if we elected as president the comments section of every terrible online article. We took our collective drunk, racist uncles and put him in the Oval Office. We set ourselves back a-yet-to-be-determined number of years as a country by giving in to our worst and most basic tendencies. And we did it all in front of our kids.

Make no mistake, our kids are watching, and they're soaking this in like sponges. It's not all about Trump, either. Listening to progressive Democrats swear up and down that they want a woman to be president but then refer to Hillary Clinton as "shrill" or claiming that all of the female presidential candidates have an "electability" problem is frustrating and hypocritical beyond belief. The fact remains that everything *feels* more polarized now because the issues we're discussing aren't just political—they're representative of our values as a society.

If you're a parent who is currently bringing up young children during these watershed times of Trump's presidency, you have even more cause to be vigilant and to talk about politics openly with your kids. This isn't just immigration we're talking about; it's whether we're okay with family separation and locking kids up in cages. It's not just Supreme Court nominations at stake; it's literally the ability of women to control their own reproductive health decisions. It's not just agreeing or disagreeing on environmental policy decisions; it's recognizing we're at a tipping point regarding climate change that will determine the sustainability of the planet for the current generation. Not to mention that young people today are paying special attention to how messages of these environmental issues are being treated, specifically Greta Thunberg, the seventeen-year-old Swedish climate change activist who has been repeatedly mocked by the President of the United States for her outspoken nature. It's also impossible to ignore the fact that transgender soldiers are no longer deemed fit to serve in our military, while discrimination protections don't apply to members of the LGBTQ+ community in certain states due to religious exemptions. The point is parents who say they don't want to talk about politics or controversial topics are really saying they don't want to talk about issues that impact all of us—and these issues are too important to society and to our kids for us to remain silent.

Perhaps the number one complaint I get on my social media channels and website is "I followed you for parenting stuff, not politics, so stick to talking about fatherhood." But that, my friends, is utter crap. You can't separate politics from parenting because politics impacts everything we do in society. The laws that govern us, the policies under which we have to live—it's all political, and it's all going to come up in the course of raising children.

So, let's just dive right into what is arguably the most important and heartbreaking issue in America today—gun culture and mass shootings.

PARENTING TIP #25: Don't let boys fall victim to gun culture

Three mass shootings occurred during the time it took for me to write this chapter. *Three.* All of the shooters were men. There can be no more whistling by the graveyard when it comes to men and mass shootings, and parents need to know that male anger and the inability to deal with rejection or meet society's masculine ideals is resulting in violent deaths.

"Because I'm really angry."

That's what nineteen-year-old Santino William Legan reportedly said when someone in attendance at the Gilroy Garlic Festival asked him why he was going on a shooting spree, which resulted in the deaths of three people, including a six-year-old boy. According to news reports, Legan bought an AK-47-style weapon just before the July 2019 incident (in neighboring Nevada, where the gun laws are more lax than California), referenced a neo-Nazi manifesto that targeted women and minorities on Instagram, sneaked through a fence, and started gunning people down before police killed him. But not before a witness, quoted by multiple news outlets, shouted out, "Why are you doing this?", to which Legan issued the horrifyingly chilling but all-too-common answer. "Because I'm really angry."[45]

I was putting together this chapter in July 2019 when this tragedy occurred, and truth be told, I was struggling mightily with the writing. Every statistic out there tells a story we already know—that the overwhelmingly majority of mass shootings are perpetrated by men. Most of them white men. Many of them angry. Angry at minorities who they see as taking over society and taking what's theirs (El Paso Walmart shooting). Angry at women for not paying them enough attention or not sleeping with them on command (Tallahassee yoga studio shooting). Just . . . angry. But while I can cite statistics all day long, I was

---

45 Matthew Ormseth, Hannah Fry, Laura Nelson, Colleen Shalby, Richard Winton, Alene Tchekmedyian, "Disturbing Portrait Emerges of Gilroy Garlic Festival Shooter," *Los Angeles Times*, July 30, 2019, https://www.latimes.com/california/story/2019-07-29/gilroy-garlic-festival-shooting-suspect

struggling to properly convey just how much our warped gun culture and gun violence are very much a male problem that ties in directly to toxic masculinity and how men view themselves in the world. I must've started and then deleted this chapter twenty times because I couldn't get it right. And then came Santino William Legan and his white male anger.

When searching for a common denominator in mass shootings, a lot of people go right to mental illness. But a University of Texas research study from February 2019 found that "counter to a lot of public opinion, having a mental illness does not necessarily make a person more likely to commit gun violence" and that "a better indicator of gun violence was access to firearms."[46] However, the one thing that can't be denied when examining gun violence (and violent crimes in general) is that almost all of the attacks are carried out by men. An FBI report from 2014 titled "A Study of Active Shooter Incidents in the United States Between 2000 and 2013" found that of 160 such incidents, only six were committed by women.[47] That means more than 96 percent of those incidents saw men pulling the trigger. This makes gun violence very much a problem perpetrated by men.

Not many people want to talk about this generation of men that is killing others and themselves, though. It's much easier to blame it all on mental illness instead of acknowledging how our culture of toxic masculinity turns boys into men who are unfeeling, robotic, and completely lacking in coping mechanisms. That's

---

46 University of Texas Medical Branch at Galveston, "Mental Illness Not to Blame for Gun Violence, Study Finds," *ScienceDaily*, February 7, 2019, https://www.sciencedaily.com/releases/2019/02/190207102607.htm

47 Pete Blair, Katherine Schweit, "A Study of Active Shooter Incidents in the United States Between 2000 and 2013," *Federal Bureau of Investigation*, 2014, https://www.fbi.gov/file-repository/active-shooter-study-2000-2013-1.pdf/view

probably why, according to a report by the Harvard T. H. Chan School of Public Health, men are four times as likely to commit suicide compared to women.[48] Meanwhile, the American Foundation for Suicide Prevention found that nearly 51 percent of suicides in 2017 involved firearms.[49] And you know what the craziest thing is? It seems to me we already know the answer.

We raise our boys to be tough at all costs. They are not allowed to cry. They are mocked and ridiculed if they openly express their feelings. They are told to be strong and silent and to never seek help, because "real men" figure things out on their own. They are told to be dominant and aggressive in sports, work, dating, and life in general. Then, after we've stunted their development as fully formed human beings and made them incapable of having any kind of wherewithal to be emotionally intelligent and competent, know what we do? We arm them.

Yup, we create hypermasculine male automatons and raise them in a toxic stew soaked with misogyny and stoked by racism, but we give them none of the tools to understand or cope with their surroundings. Eventually, they succumb to these alpha male attitudes, and the bullied become the bullies. Then, somewhere along the way, we hand them one of the 300 million guns in circulation today. Then we make ownership of said gun a central component to their manhood, and suddenly, confused and angry-as-fuck men are now holding legally purchased killing machines as they hop onto Reddit and 8chan to discuss far-right manifestos and blame women and minorities for everything that hasn't gone right in their lives. And when all that violence and

---

48 Madeline Drexler, "Guns and Suicide: The Hidden Toll," *Harvard Public Health*, accessed September 15, 2019, https://www.hsph.harvard.edu/magazine/magazine_article/guns-suicide/

49 "Suicide Statistics," American Foundation for Suicide Prevention, accessed September 15, 2019, https://afsp.org/about-suicide/suicide-statistics/

anger in which they've been raised finally bubbles to the surface, and these men have no idea what a healthy coping mechanism looks like, it becomes easier just to grab the gun—which will only end in two possible ways, and neither of them are good.

To make things worse is how we talk about guns, shootings, and the cause of all the violence *after* it happens, as if we don't already know the answer. What do we do as a society when these men blow up and hurt themselves and/or others? We throw our hands up in feigned confusion and shout to the heavens, *"Why is this happening?"* and *"What could possibly make someone do this?"* Well, you have most of your answer. This happens because of a confluence of events and factors that are part and parcel of the toxicity in which we raise men, combined with an embarrassingly easy access to guns in this country. This is the reason you see so few female shooters. This is the inevitable conclusion to the terrible way we box men in emotionally and raise them in what amounts to a microwave that blasts and cooks together toxic masculinity, misogyny, and white supremacy.

I disagree completely with those of you who say, "It's mental illness, dumbass!", or who blame violent video games for gun violence. Countries all over the world contain people who suffer from mental illness; and kids from all nationalities are playing Grand Theft Auto and other video games. Also, both men and women are susceptible to mental illness. Yet, despite the fact, they are not shooting up malls, grocery stores, and music festivals with the appalling frequency of the incidents in the United States. Why? Because of the inordinate number of guns the United States has in circulation, the embarrassingly lax background checks in far too many states to own one, and this country's uniquely warped gun culture and version of masculinity. I understand it's easier to blame the mental health boogeyman, but doing so only ignores the actual problem of how intrinsically intertwined masculinity and gun ownership is.

And if you think that gun companies don't already realize this and actively tap into it, then let me tell you a tale about how one gun company advertised to men for two years prior to the Sandy Hook Elementary School shooting in Newtown, Connecticut.

In 2010, Bushmaster Firearms began an advertising campaign that will long live in my mind as the gold standard of poisonous, dangerous, and irresponsible marketing. That was the year the company began running promotions that featured an AR-15 rifle with five simple words splayed across the front: "Consider Your Man Card Reissued."[50] The implication is quite clear—if you're a real man (and you can always tell the real ones from the fake ones because they have their handy dandy Man Card at the ready), you own a gun. If you don't own a gun, well, then have a seat on the bench, Sally. Because what could go wrong by insinuating you need to own a weapon that can fire thirty bullets in rapid succession to rightfully consider yourself masculine?

But wait, there's more.

Bushmaster took things a step further by creating the Man Card Online promotion, which consisted of an online quiz in which test-takers were asked a series of complex and Mensa-level questions meant to gauge their manhood and ultimately determine if they were truly worthy of possessing the much-sought-after Man Card. It was (so originally) called "The Man Test," and the copy read as follows: "It's game time, Sunshine. The simple man test that follows is all that stands between you and a return to man

---

50 Emma Gray, "Bushmaster Rifle Ad Reminds Us to Ask More About Masculinity and Gun Violence," *Huffington Post*, December 17, 2012, https://www.huffpost.com/entry/bushmaster-rifle-ad-masculinity-gun-violence-newtown-adam-lanza_b_2317924

glory. Search your soul. Answer honestly. And let the truth decide your fate." Men taking this test know upfront that Bushmaster isn't messing around, because their "man glory" is at stake.

What are the questions, you ask? "Do you think tofu is an acceptable meat?" Holy shit. Don't get me wrong, I don't like tofu, either, but not because eating it chips away at my fragile male ego and renders me unworthy of man glory. God help you if you answered *yes* to that question, because real men wouldn't be caught dead eating a healthier meat substitute that's better for your long-term health instead of a raw, bloody cow (even though I think tofu tastes like sadness).

The next question is multiple choice: "A carload of rival fans deliberately cuts you off in traffic on the way to the championship game. What do you do?" Your choices are: "A: I slump down in my seat and change the music on the stereo, hoping the guys with me in my car don't notice the slight. B: I start singing the fight song of my own team in a high, merry voice. C: I skip the game, find the other car in the parking lot, and render it unrecognizable with a conflagration of shoe polish and empty food containers. D: I ignore their rudeness, assuming it's just a mistake, despite the team flags flying from my car windows." There's a lot to unpack in this one. As you might imagine, ignoring the unforgivable travesty of being cut off in traffic and calming down with music or turning the other cheek isn't going to get you to Man Glory anytime soon. No sir. And singing the fight song—especially in a high, merry voice, which is feminine and therefore unacceptable—is no good, either. Clearly the only Man-Card-level solution is to go after the bastards and commit vandalism.

Let's not forget this is a gun company that's part of the gun industry with a goal of having as many people as possible own as many guns as possible in as many places as possible. And surely the fine folks at Bushmaster know road rage is a very real, very dangerous thing, especially where guns are involved. Yet, there they are, a gun company telling men that a real man would risk starting a confrontation with potentially armed parties all because they were cut off in traffic. That shit is flat-out disgusting and morally repugnant in every way. It's also wildly irresponsible as it dares men to commit crimes.

I don't have to tell you that it keeps going. "What of these best expresses your inner light?" The choices were between a very cute kitten, an AR-15, and a lovely votive candle. (Obviously you can't pick the cat; the candle is slightly confusing because fire is wicked masculine, but it's a clear fuck-no-bro to chick candles; the choice here is clear—nothing expresses a man's inner light like the flashes from the muzzle when you're shooting shit.) "You blow a tire on the highway. Do you know where to look for your jack and your spare?" Bushmaster might as well ask if you know where to look to find your balls, because if you answer *no* to this question, you won't need them anyway. (This might be a good time to mention that I don't know shit about cars; meanwhile, my wife embarrassed me on our first date when she successfully restarted her brother's broken-down jeep when I panicked and misdiagnosed the problem as having to do with "an engine rotator splint" in hopes of impressing her. The good news is today, I've freed myself from the unnecessary shame and guilt that toxic masculinity demands men have when it comes to automotive repair knowledge—I give zero fucks that I don't know a thing because I know my wife can handle it.)

Finally, if you "pass" Bushmaster's Man Test, it reads, "You've redeemed your man priveleges [sic]" (because spelling is for wimps who haven't mastered the intricacies of the AR-15). "Now prove it! Print, send or post your Man Card!" After all, you're not truly a man until you've whipped it out and shown it to everyone, right? Also, just in case you needed an ignorant cherry on top of this toxic sundae, Bushmaster had a way for dudes to call for the revocation of someone else's Man Card. It's hard to believe the surely peer-reviewed and scientifically sound theory behind Bushmaster's Man Test could possibly be wrong, but just in case, they allowed men to enter the information of other men whose manliness they wanted to call into question. Under the "What's the problem?" field, men could choose from "Crybaby," "Cupcake," "Short Leash," "Coward," and "Just Unmanly." In the next field, you could get into the specifics of why this man should be served a revocation notice: "Actually ordered an appletini with other men present"; "Does Pilates regularly"; "Has a dog so small it can fit in his wallet"; "Gets haircuts that cost more than eight bucks"; "Decries the eating of red meat while extolling the virtues of soy-based substitutes for pretty much everything else on Earth"; "Has a bumper sticker on his car complaining about 'mean people'"; "Avoids eye contact with tough looking fifth-graders"; and "Wears hemp clothing with no sense of embarrassment."

To me, Bushmaster's test is a clear indication of the link between seemingly innocuous "jokes" that perpetuate gender stereotypes and the reality of gun culture and the violence it creates. Even though some will say this was just an advertising campaign, it really went beyond that—it took all the anger and violence involved in being male and weaponized it with the sole purpose of shaming men into owning guns to be more "manly." And it did so at the expense of women, not only because "feminine" traits and activities were treated as bad things to be avoided at all costs in the test, but also because women have long been on the receiving end of male gun violence (and domestic violence in general).

In an article in the May/June 2019 issue of Crime & Justice in *MotherJones* titled "Armed and Misogynist: How Toxic Masculinity Fuels Mass Shootings," author Mark Follman examined mass shootings since 2011 and found "a stark pattern of misogyny and domestic violence among many attackers" and "a strong overlap between toxic masculinity and public mass shootings." He wrote, "Based on case documents, media reports, and interviews with mental health and law enforcement experts, we found that in at least 22 mass shootings since 2011—more than a third of the public attacks over the past eight years—the perpetrators had a history of domestic violence, specifically targeted women, or had stalked and harassed women. These cases included the large-scale massacres at an Orlando nightclub in 2016 and a church in Sutherland Springs, Texas, in 2017. In total, they account for 175 victims killed and 158 others injured. Two of the shooters bore the hallmarks of so-called 'incels'—a subculture of virulent misogynists who self-identify as 'involuntarily celibate' and voice their rage and revenge fantasies against women online. A man who recently planned to carry out a mass shooting in Utah and another who opened fire outside a courthouse in Dallas also appeared to be influenced by incel ideas."[51]

Let me make one thing very clear from the outset—none of this is an excuse for men who target and kill women. It is just vital that we consider the societal factors that lead to these incidents so we can learn more about how to prevent them. From the research, a laundry list of examples demonstrates it's a certain kind of misogynistic, angry, bigoted, and toxic man who

---

51 Mark Follman, "Armed and Misogynist: How Toxic Masculinity Fuels Mass Shootings," *Mother Jones*, May/June 2019 issue, https://www.motherjones.com/crime-justice/2019/06/domestic-violence-misogyny-incels-mass-shootings/

becomes a shooter. Furthermore, they often leave behind furious manifestos and display copious warning signs before taking the extreme step of murdering people in cold blood, because they either couldn't deal with their anger or felt that the taking of life was the only way to truly feel powerful in a world that never saw them as the masculine ideal—which is sadly ironic since the "masculine ideal" is a cultural construct that lies to us in the first place.

The most notorious example of an incel who turned deadly is Elliot Rodger. In May 2014, Rodger killed six people on the University of California, Santa Barbara campus and injured fourteen others before turning the gun on himself. Rodger self-identified as an incel, leaving behind a 137-page manifesto along with YouTube videos calling for revenge on all the women who had rejected him (even though he never talked to most of them). Rodger was a bullied boy who believed wealth was inexorably tied to acceptance, and he grew to despise happy couples and loathed other boys who could be easily social and attract attention from the "hot blondes" he coveted. Because he had no idea how to cope with these feelings, he'd simply withdraw, skipping school to lose himself in World of Warcraft for weeks rather than deal with real life. The two things that he believed made a man a man—sex and money—were elusive to him. When he couldn't gain attention from women, he turned to the pursuit of riches, spending thousands of dollars on lottery tickets, believing that if he were suddenly rich, he'd be drowning in women. Each time he lost, he sunk deeper into a tailspin of depression and toxicity, until he tried unsuccessfully to break in to a sorority house and settled for shooting women outside the house instead. The rantings from his manifesto reveal his warped reasoning for the shooting, the hate he was harboring for women, and the pain he felt at not fitting into the traditional model of masculinity—he resolved to destroy everything he believed he couldn't have.[52]

And he's far from alone in feeling this way.

In October 2015, Chris Harper-Mercer killed nine people and injured eight others before killing himself in a shooting at Umpqua Community College in Oregon. In his manifesto left for police at the scene, he looked up to other incel shooters like Rodger but criticized them for not killing more people. Like Rodger, he thought of himself as a loser who had nothing to live for and believed that he had failed to achieve the successes in life that he considered masculine. "My whole life has been one lonely enterprise. One loss after another. And here I am, 26, with no friends, no job, no girlfriend, a virgin," he wrote.[53]

Scott Beierle killed two women in a yoga studio and injured four more in November 2018 after mentioning Rodger in videos on YouTube. An admitted member of the incel community, Beierle was also a military veteran and a substitute teacher who was fired from one job for allegedly asking a female student if she was ticklish and then touching her just below her bra line. He also had a history of arrests for grabbing women by their posteriors. In a familiar fit of irony, he would routinely talk of his intense hatred for women, but then in the next breath lament

---

52 Christina Warren, "Elliot Rodger: Portrait of a Lonely Outcast Obsessed with Status," *Mashable*, May 25, 2014, https://mashable.com/2014/05/25/elliot-rodger-profile/

53 Rick Anderson, "'Here I am, 26, with no friends, no job, no girlfriend': Shooter's manifesto offers clues to 2015 Oregon college rampage," *Los Angeles Times*, September 23, 2017, https://www.latimes.com/nation/la-na-school-shootings-2017-story.html

the fact that he didn't have a girlfriend.[54] Likewise, in December 2017, William Atchison killed two people before killing himself in New Mexico in a shooting at Aztec High School, where he had previously been a student. He had used the pseudonym "Elliot Rodger" and "Adam Lanza" (the Newtown, Connecticut, shooter) on several online forums, talked glowingly about the Columbine school shooting and praised Rodger and the incel community.[55] Even Nikolas Cruz, the Parkland school shooter in Florida who killed seventeen people at Stoneman Douglas High School had previously written an online post saying "Elliot Rodger will not be forgotten."[56]

Our current society is set up for men (especially white men) to thrive—because that's who built the system. Men are set up to be the kings of the universe, who make $500,000 a year and are rolling in women. So our boys see what society expects from them, and it's not surprising that when boys start to struggle socially as they try to meet these unrealistic standards, they are shocked when they can't meet that bar. And because they're also supposed to be emotional islands unto themselves who never ask for help and who must remain tough at all costs, they are unable to work through their isolation and emotional toxicity to learn healthy coping mechanisms. Therefore, when confronted

---

54 Bob D'Angelo, "Who Was Scott Beierle, the Shooter at the Tallahassee Yoga Shop," *Atlanta Journal Constitution*, November 4, 2018, https://www.ajc.com/news/who-was-scott-beierle-the-shooter-the-tallahassee-yoga-shop/RnAVWFBLNHzv8zzSXaqQnN/

55 Brandy Zadrozny, Ben Collins, "New Mexico School Shooter Had Secret Life on Pro-Trump White-Supremacy Sites," *The Daily Beast*, December 15, 2017, https://www.thedailybeast.com/new-mexico-school-shooter-had-secret-life-on-pro-trump-white-supremacy-sites

56 Ben Collions, Brandy Zadrozny, "After Toronto Attack, Online Misogynists Praise Suspect as 'New Saint'," *NBC News*, April 24, 2018, https://www.nbcnews.com/news/us-news/after-toronto-attack-online-misogynists-praise-suspect-new-saint-n868821

with any kind of failure that threatens their fragile male ego, they resort to the only thing they know and have been taught— intense anger. Then anger turns to violence.

Shortly before writing this chapter, my oldest son started dating his first girlfriend. It did not go well, and in true sixth grade fashion, it was over before it even started and she broke up with him. So, I checked in on him to gauge how he was feeling and to teach him healthy ways to deal with his feelings. I told him people break up for all kinds of reasons, and that while it can be painful, it's also a part of life. I reminded him that there would also be times in the future when he might need to break up with people, and that he should do so with respect while valuing the other person's dignity (even if the people in your past don't extend you the same courtesy). We talked about how even though he wanted her back, it was important to respect her decision and to not stalk her on social media or in real life because boundaries are essential. It all sounds like simple common sense, but how many parents actually have these conversations with their sons? I'll bet it's a shockingly low percentage, and as these boys grow into men, we'll see a society that reflects this lack of vital communication.

Look, I'm not against responsible gun ownership, and I don't believe in banning all guns; I have friends who hunt and who have taken me to the gun range, and it's been fun. Groups like the National Rifle Association want to turn this into a Second Amendment debate, but parents need to know that's separate from what we're talking about here. Please talk to your sons about learning to deal with rejection in a healthy way. Talk to them about self-reflection and not blaming women for all of their woes. Discuss how vapid and superficial society's norms are for men and point them in the direction of healthier alternatives.

And if they really need it, get them counseling. If not, angry boys turn into angry men who still can't deal with rejection—but who can meet the requirements to legally carry. I believe the most effective way we can battle gun violence is for parents of boys to start talking with them at an early age and help them avoid the rigid, harmful constraints of toxic masculinity that lead to a nearly all-male cast of mass shooters. Because that statistic is not a coincidence, and it cannot be ignored any longer.

PARENTING TIP #26: Embrace politics and discuss them with your kids

Just as height, hair color, and eye color are determined by genetics, so is politics, at least when your kids are still young—you have a very high chance of passing on your political views to your children. Kids are sponges and parents are their heroes, so they're going to believe what you believe and they're going to parrot your viewpoints in public and at school. You need to truly sit down and understand the ramifications of little people having outsized opinions that they don't yet fully comprehend and that they may shout over the playground, because I can tell you with 100 percent certainty that it doesn't just affect you; it impacts all of us. Once you're aware of this, you can act accordingly.

Case in point, Will was seven years old and in the second grade when the 2016 presidential election kicked into high gear. Trump had kicked off his presidential bid by calling some Mexicans rapists and promising to build a border wall that Mexico would magically pay for, which began the intense and frequent vilification of immigrants and the day Will came home from school and said something that floored us. "Mom, Dad . . . you know how you told me about Trump and the Wall and people coming across the border? I think it's fine if they get in line and ask permission to come in, but if they try to sneak in, then Trump has to shoot them to protect us, right?" My wife and I were stunned, and the horrified looks on our faces spooked him because he immediately started to get upset and backtrack. "I mean, I'm not talking about shooting the good ones. Just the ones trying to sneak in because those are the terrorists."

We had told him most immigrants are hard workers who come here for a better life but through TV and friends he had absorbed "people crossing the border illegally are terrorists who have to be shot to protect the USA." How did Will make this stunning 180-degree turn? It turned out a couple of other kids in his class—and let me remind you that we're talking about kids in *second grade*—had told him those very words because they had heard it from their dads.

We sat a very upset and confused Will down (again) and talked to him about how important it is to understand that immigrants are not terrorists and that they do not deserve to be shot. This experience was a sobering one for me because it taught me a few important things about kids, parenting, and politics. First, kids will take whatever their parents say and use it in the way that makes the most sense to them. Second, an alarming amount of good parenting can be undone in a terrifyingly short amount of time by classmates and friends. And finally, the things we say as parents, even in the privacy of our own homes, will find an audience outside of those walls. If you're a parent who is a xenophobic proponent of walls, it doesn't matter if you don't express that viewpoint publicly. If you do it in front of your kid, you must acknowledge that your views will be shared with the world one way or another. That is an awesome responsibility, and it's one I wish parents would think about more often.

I'm also not ashamed to tell you that I've made a decision as a parent to disallow my children from hanging out with kids whose parents I know hold hateful views. This is a very sore issue in the parenting community, and many people believe I'm the one who is discriminating based on political views. But what we need to remember is these are not ordinary times. This isn't a case of simply having opposing political views or policy differences. I disagreed on many, many issues when it came to past Republican nominees like John McCain and Mitt Romney, but even if they had won the presidency, I wouldn't have been worried about the state of America. I wouldn't be having a constant concern that our society is falling apart at the seams. I wouldn't cringe every time I get on Twitter, out of fear of seeing the President of the United States tell a US citizen and Congresswoman of color to go back to Africa, while his pack of sycophantic "patriots" cheer and chant, "lock her up" and "send her back." I wouldn't be preventing my kids from hanging out with other kids whose parents do not share my politics. But the fact of the matter is we're very much in uncharted territory, and I have a responsibility to bring my kids up in a healthy, safe environment that is about love, not hate. My kids and their values are too important for me to knowingly expose them to the dangerous and unhealthy toxicity of our times.

Some people will say, "Well, aren't you just brainwashing your son with liberal ideas?" As I've mentioned, my kids will likely inherit my political views on the world anyway, and they'll always have the chance to decide for themselves as they grow up and face the world. What's important to me now is making sure I bring up my kids to be respectful, supportive, and compassionate. And by my definition, that means teaching them to fully support the rights for gay people to marry, as well as to be ardent supporters of trans rights. It means teaching them that while open borders aren't the answer, a path to citizenship and humane treatment shouldn't involve families separated and putting kids in cages. It means teaching them to advocate for equal pay for women and supporting common-sense gun laws. If my kids understand the simple concepts of consent and bodily autonomy for women to make their own reproductive health decisions, then I know I'm also bringing them up to be compassionate members of society. And my hope is that kids like mine will rub off on kids like the ones in Will's second-grade classroom, instead of the other way around.

Not to mention these "political" discussions strike at the very heart of who people are and even how they identify. For example, the proper use of gendered pronouns have become a political hot button, and if you're a parent who thinks you can whistle by the graveyard on this issue, you've got another thing coming. We now know that human sexuality is fluid, and kids are identifying in a variety of ways beyond he/him and she/her. While there are those who think political correctness and "PC culture" is nothing more than thought-policing people with more conservative viewpoints, why not teach your kids that respecting someone enough to identify them the way they feel most comfortable is simply common courtesy? Just as it's no longer respectful to call Asian people *orientals* or use the word *retard* when talking about developmentally disabled people, it costs nothing to be kind to someone who wishes to be referred to as *they/them*.

Instead of desperately trying to avoid these "political" issues simply because they're sensitive and they make you uncomfortable, it's vital to get past that. Tackle these truly important topics head on because your kids will have to do the same very soon. Plus, if you don't discuss it with your kids, trust me, they'll hear it from someone else, and that gets real messy real fast.

PARENTING TIP #27: Teach boys (especially white boys) about privilege

I was in my early twenties when I first heard the phrase *white privilege*, and I didn't like it one bit. Same for *male privilege*. As a straight white man, it made me feel like I couldn't have a say in things or that I should feel guilty for the sins of my forefathers, with which I had nothing to do. So, I did what many other heterosexual, white males do when confronted with this topic—I dismissed it and made fun of the person delivering the message. It took the internet and joining a community of fathers from around the world who look very different from me and who talk openly and honestly about their experiences to turn me around on this important topic. Which, again, was not an easy thing. I despise having to admit I'm wrong, and holy hell, did I have to eat a ton of crow when it came to admitting the existence of privilege and coming to grips with the fact that I benefit from it daily. I'm perpetually grateful to the men in my life who (judiciously) told me what a blind idiot I was, because that lesson came just in time for me to teach my own boys about privilege.

What is white male privilege? The best way I have ever seen this explained is from a 2012 essay by John Scalzi titled "Straight White Male: The Lowest Difficulty Setting There Is," in which he compares life to a video game everyone is playing, except straight white males are playing on the easiest setting. "This means that the default behaviors for almost all the non-player characters in the game are easier on you than they would be otherwise. The default barriers for completions of quests are lower. Your leveling-up thresholds come more quickly. You automatically gain entry to some parts of the map that others have to work for. The game is easier to play, automatically, and when you need help, by default it's easier to get."[57]

And make no mistake, you can still lose while playing on the "straight white male" setting, just like people who play on more difficult settings can win. But just because you lost on the "straight while male" setting doesn't mean the game wasn't easier for you to play. And if you did win, it doesn't diminish your accomplishments or insinuate that you didn't work as hard or play as well. All it means is you had built-in advantages, most of which you would have never even noticed if you weren't looking for them, because the game was set up to benefit you from the start. And the first step toward confronting white male privilege, if you are a white male person, is to recognize that fact. This explanation of privilege went over extremely well with my oldest, who is a devoted gamer, and he grasped what I was saying right away.

When I shared this to members of my family and my friends, some of them shook their heads and told me it wasn't appropriate to have that conversation with a young kid who had done nothing wrong in the first place. Their argument was that he didn't have a racist or misogynistic bone in his body, and the best thing we can do for our kids is to teach them to be colorblind and genderblind. They firmly believe, most of them with the best of intentions, that teaching kids not to see racial or gender differences is the way to go and the path to a truly enlightened society.

I understand where they're coming from, but I disagree with that completely and vehemently.

It's important to talk to boys about privilege because they need to understand our society's problems before they can fix

---

57 John Scalzi, "Straight White Male: The Lowest Difficulty Setting There Is," *kotaku.com*, May 17, 2012, https://kotaku.com/straight-white-male-the-lowest-difficulty-setting-ther-5910857

them. My boys need to know they will be paid more for doing the same job as women simply because they are men. They also need to know they are thirty percent more likely to be interviewed for that job in the first place because they have white-sounding names.[58] I'm going to teach them about systemic racism and inherent gender bias because I need them to see and understand that differences in ethnicity and sex matter in this world, even though we wish they didn't. Teaching white boys to be color-blind or blind to gender differences might be well-intentioned, but unfortunately it will lead to them being blind to the real-life disparities that will occur specifically because of these differences. Also, awareness of these discrepancies means parents can teach kids to advocate for marginalized peoples in a variety of ways. Whether it's recognizing and calling out microaggressions; standing up to bullies who benefit from a systemic power structure; or even making the decision to purchase books, art, and cinematic entertainment created by underrepresented minorities, the recognition of privilege is a stepping stone to actions that directly benefit these communities.

Some people today will argue that there is no such thing as white male privilege, that the gender wage gap is a myth, and that we live in a post-racial society where meritocracy rules the day and everyone is on a level-playing field. They'll also tell you that the entire concept of privilege is political correctness run amok, and they'll point to #MeToo and all the famous white men brought down by recent scandals to flip the script and say it's actually really difficult to be a white, straight man in society

---

58 Bertrand, Marianne and Sendhil Mullainathan. "Are Emily And Greg More Employable Than Lakisha And Jamal? A Field Experiment On Labor Market Discrimination," *American Economic Review*, 2004, v94(4,Sep), 991-1013.

today, who is constantly under attack. Don't listen to them, and don't let your children be affected by these beliefs, because that is bullshit. The people who claim they are under attack are those who have finally been uncomfortably awoken to the fact that they can no longer continue getting away with *getting away with things*, like sexual harassment. And while these people are upset about a loss of privilege and having to reckon with their behaviors, the truth is black people were only granted the right to vote 150 years ago, while women earned the vote just 100 years ago. People of color didn't truly earn anything resembling equal status until just more than 50 years ago with the Civil Rights Movement. In the span of human history, that is akin to yesterday. The effects of slavery still reverberate to this day, and women are still playing catch-up as well. Heterosexual white men have always enjoyed the systemic advantages set up and maintained by their straight white peers in power, and they will likely continue to do so well into the future. Our boys need to know this reality if they're going to be able to help change things for the better. It's common sense and essential to teach children while they are young, so we can begin to change the system from its roots.

Parents of white, straight boys can have these difficult conversations in gentle ways that doesn't make them feel ashamed of being any of those things, while helping them understand they're the beneficiaries of certain societal advantages not everyone else enjoys. Without that knowledge, they risk growing up and becoming people who feel like they're losing equality simply because other people are gaining theirs.

PARENTING TIP #28: Talk to boys about bodily autonomy and boundaries

As parents, do you make your kids give people hugs? Grandparents, aunts, uncles—they all want hugs and kisses from little kids, and many aren't shy about demanding them. I understand there's a tendency to give in and tell your children to go over and provide adults with physical affection. I sure as hell didn't think about any potential negative repercussions—not when I was a kid and not when I first became a parent. I was made to hug and kiss my relatives, even when I didn't feel like it, so I carried on with that mindset with my own children.

But forcing children to provide physical affection to adults on-demand is not a good idea, says Dr. Jack Levine, an executive committee member on developmental and behavioral pediatrics at the American Academy of Pediatrics, because you're taking away a child's say in who they give affection to.[59] And it makes sense—adults aren't made to hug one another if they don't want to, so why should kids not be extended the same courtesy? Granted, this can make things awkward at family gatherings if your kids decide they don't want to give someone a hug, and some of your relatives might not take kindly to a perceived snub. But that discomfort pales in comparison to upholding bodily autonomy for your kids and allowing them to maintain their boundaries.

In fact, this is a precursor to future conversations with your child about the importance of consent, and it dovetails with the conversations you should already be having, even with young kids, about not letting anyone touch them if they're not comfortable with it. Looking back, I felt foolish for telling my kids

---

59 Robin Young, "Don't Force Your Kids to Hug and Kiss Relatives During the Holidays, Pediatrician Says," *WBUR*, Dec. 3, 2018, https://www.wbur.org/hereandnow/2018/12/03/forced-affection-holidays-kids-family

that no one could touch them if they didn't want to be touched but then getting angry and forcing them to hug and kiss people when they really didn't want to. For someone who values consistency, I was sending out quite the mixed message. It also sets up for a possibly problematic future scenario if a loved one or an authority figure ultimately becomes abusive in some way—if you've told your kids they have to hug and kiss someone, and that same person begins an abusive relationship, you've left that child at a decided disadvantage because they already feel they lack the agency to say no. It's the same reason we have a rule at our house about tickling—if someone says "stop," then it stops right then and there. I know it seems very mundane, and some might assume we have absolutely no fun at our house, but the fact of the matter is I can't have more serious conversations with my kids about bodily autonomy and consent if I'm forcing them to give physical affection to other people against their will.

It's also something boys can easily internalize and take in an unfortunate direction. If they see little girls being forced to provide people with physical affection even when they've said no, that becomes a baseline and a norm that can carry over into how they view romantic relationships later on in life—even on a subconscious level. It reinforces the mistaken belief that even if girls don't want to provide intimacy, they have to if they're told. And frankly, I believe it's one of the factors in play regarding male politicians and how they seek to restrict bodily autonomy for women in the form of abortion legislation.

I should admit, right off the bat, that this is a very personal topic for me. In 2010, my wife MJ and I were trying for our second child, and we endured three miscarriages. When we got one that stuck, we anxiously sat on the news until the traditional twelve-week mark when the risks of loss plummet dramatically. I remember weeping tears of joy during the ultrasound and squeezing MJ's hand because we had finally made it through all that loss, and soon we'd give Will the brother or sister he so desperately wanted. And we were due on New Year's Eve, no less. Then came the dreaded call from the radiologist, telling us he'd like us to come in for one more "precautionary" ultrasound because he had noticed something about the baby's legs.

At sixteen weeks, we found out our baby had Sirenomelia, also known as Mermaid Syndrome, where the legs are fused together. Worse than that, the baby was missing vital organs needed for survival outside the womb, such as kidneys, an anus, and a bladder. Doctors told us the condition occurs in 1 out of every 100,000 pregnancies. While our baby was still alive and had a remote chance of living until birth, we were told there was "zero chance" for survival outside the womb. In an instant, we went from our plans of being a family of four to having to choose between waiting two weeks until they could get us into the hospital in Boston, at which point we ran the risk of MJ having to deliver a stillborn, or going to an affiliated clinic for an abortion.

We took a day to consider which of the two impossibly heartbreaking options we wanted to run with, as if it were the worst Choose Your Own Adventure Book on the planet. In the end, MJ and I opted for what we believe was the most merciful option for our baby—the abortion. The thought of waiting another two weeks with a dying baby inside of her and then potentially having to deliver said baby stillborn was too much for MJ to bear. On the day of the procedure we pulled into the Brookline clinic, and there they were—religious anti-choice zealots set up on the perimeter of the property, holding up signs featuring unborn children and screaming at people entering the clinic. These people, who didn't know us or our situation, woke up that day and decided the best use of their time was to shame perfect strangers on one of the toughest days of their lives for making a perfectly legal and safe reproductive health decision. A decision, by the way, that was absolutely none of their business. I wrapped my arm around MJ and whispered, "Ignore these ignorant fucks," but even with the thirty-five-foot buffer zone that was in place at the time (and has since been declared unconstitutional) across busy Harvard Avenue, we heard them. The last thing we heard as we entered the clinic was how we were murdering our unborn baby.

As soon as we got in the door through security, MJ lost it. She broke. And let me tell you, despite not believing in the version of Hell with Satan and pitchforks, I discovered that day that hell is actually real. Not only that, it's right here on Earth. Spend twenty minutes watching the love of your life moan and wail and convulse with sobs right before she goes in to literally have a life taken out of her, and you'll come to the same conclusion. I stood there, helpless, as she was further tortured by informed consent laws that stipulate doctors are legally obligated to describe the procedure in excruciating detail even if you've already read up on it. Even if you tearfully beg them to stop talking. I felt my heart break into a million pieces as I watched her taken away to a surgery room where I couldn't accompany her to comfort her. So yes, there's a hell. And the people outside that clinic inexplicably help make it a reality by unnecessarily and cruelly shaming women.

I was a newspaper reporter at the time, and I knew my rights inside and out. I knew they were on a public sidewalk and absolutely had the right to say whatever they wanted. But I knew I could peacefully exercise my First Amendment rights as well. So, I took out my phone and started recording as I walked up to them and asked why they were doing what they were doing.

I explained our situation and watched them flounder around for some kind of rationale for their terrible behavior. I listened to them babble on about suicide rates for women who get abortions. And then, in an amazing fit of irony, I watched as they threatened to call the police on me for recording them on a public sidewalk, as if their free speech was the only speech that is protected.

By the time I picked MJ up, the police were there, though the protesters had gone. MJ groggily asked, "What did you do?" with a wry, tired smile. Later that day (with MJ's permission), I uploaded the video on YouTube and my website, where it soon garnered more than a million views and was picked up by news outlets all over the world. The reaction was swift and overwhelming, as I began hearing responses from all sides. The religious fanatics and anti-choice folks came out in droves to tell me I was a baby killer, accusing us of faking the whole thing and wishing death upon us via emails and online comments. They found my parents' phone number and called them, too, screaming at my mom and dad for raising a murderer. But on the flip side—and the reason I'd do it all over again in a heartbeat—was when I started hearing from women all across the world. Women who had had abortions in the past and who had also been viciously harassed by people who think tormenting strangers is doing God's work. Young women who couldn't tell their parents and who had to walk that gauntlet alone. Older women who had had abortions twenty, thirty, and forty years ago, but who still remember the sting of shame and guilt from their verbal assailants. No matter their age, ethnicity, or location, they all said they wish they had been strong enough to fight back that day, or that they had had someone in their lives willing to be an advocate for them against that onslaught of judgment. And while the two people I had confronted that day were female, the women who had abortions and took the time to write me all expressed bewilderment and anger over the fact that so many of their detractors had been men.

Men whose bodies are unaffected by pregnancy. Men who will never have to make that difficult decision. Men who like the idea of a baby, but who will never have to push one out of his body. Let me tell you right now—any man who actively attempts to control a woman's body by working to outlaw abortion is a misogynist.

Our boys need to know if you're a man who wants to make abortion illegal, then you're someone who wants to punish women for maintaining control of her own body. Look, no one likes abortion. Despite what the religious right would have you believe, women who get abortions and the men who support them are not throwing abortion parties and doling out free coat hangers on every street corner. What I'm teaching my boys is while you don't have to like abortion, you do have to value choice and bodily autonomy. Because the minute you advocate for making abortion illegal, you become an advocate for stripping women of the basic right to control their own bodies and to make the reproductive health decisions that are best for them. And if abortion becomes illegal, which means it's a crime with punishments, that means you're in favor of punishing women for making decisions about their own bodies. That's not okay. A woman's right (and really, every human's right) to control her own body should be sacrosanct, and boys and men should know they *never* have the right to dictate what someone else does with their own body.

I've talked about this topic with my oldest. He's rightly uncomfortable about getting behind an idea that ends a pregnancy, which is understandable. But I explained to him that while it's fine to be personally against abortion, it's wrong to let your personal views restrict what someone else of the opposite sex does with her body, and he understands that now. More boys need to know that a girl's body is not his to control, whether it's about reproductive decisions or even the clothes she chooses to wear.

That last point, in particular, is difficult to convey thanks to Draconian dress codes still in effect at many schools across the nation, where bare shoulders, shorts or skirts above the knee, and even leggings are outlawed. Girls are routinely singled out and forced to either change into "appropriate" clothes or leave school altogether, and the reason often given is that their outfits create a distracting environment for boys.

Parents—and I can't stress this enough—please push back against those dress codes and that mindset. When this occurs, the message we're conveying is that girls are not only responsible for their actions, but they're also responsible for the actions of boys as well. Did a boy sexually harass a girl in his class? Well, what was *she* wearing? As if her bare shoulders are an invitation or an excuse for boys to harass girls in any way, shape, or form. On the flip side, boys will continue to learn that they are not responsible for their actions because they are simply lust-fueled hormone monsters with no restraint once girls reveal even the most non-sexual parts of their bodies. Parents of boys need to hammer home the fact that boys and boys alone are responsible for their own actions. They need to know it doesn't matter if a girl comes to class naked; that still doesn't give anyone the right to assault or harass her. Boys are responsible for their own behaviors, and if they can't focus in class because they're distracted by a girl's appearance, that's on them. By making girls cover up, we are telling boys that they have the power to influence the appearance of girls, and it tells girls that their body isn't just theirs, it's subject to the whim of the male gaze.

Talk to your boys and instill in them personal accountability and the importance of boundaries and autonomy at all levels, even if it means refusing Aunt Mary for a hug.

PARENTING TIP #29: Teach boys about consent and how not to contribute to rape culture

If we want to teach our sons how to respect our daughters, we first have to talk about rape culture. Because rape culture is not just about the act of rape; it's about the culture and codes of behavior that lead men to rape, that normalize sexual violence, and that blame victims while pardoning perpetrators.

History in general has not been kind to women who have come forward with allegations of sexual impropriety by men, especially powerful men. According to a June 2019 report from ABC News, "at least 17 women have accused Donald Trump of varying inappropriate behavior, including allegations of sexual harassment or sexual assault, all but one coming forward with their accusations before or during his bid for the White House."[60] But instead of putting the full force of the law behind investigating Trump and these disturbing allegations, society has placed the spotlight and burden of responsibility on Trump's accusers. Why didn't they come forward sooner? What were they wearing at the time? What's their dating history look like?

Perhaps that shouldn't come as a surprise since former President Bill Clinton famously abused the power of his office two decades ago when he conducted an affair with White House intern Monica

---

60 Meghan Keneally, "List of Trump's Accusers and Their Allegations of Sexual Misconduct," *ABC News*, June 25, 2019, https://abcnews. go.com/Politics/list-trumps-accusers-allegations-sexual-misconduct/ story?id=51956410

Lewinsky. Although Clinton went on to be impeached (but not removed from office), it was Lewinsky who endured the brunt of the shaming despite being on the wrong end of a power differential—for tempting Clinton and engaging in a relationship with a married man. But it was Trump's infamous Access Hollywood tape, released shortly before the election, that was most jarring: "You know I'm automatically attracted to beautiful . . . I just start kissing them. It's like a magnet. Just kiss. I don't even wait. And when you're a star, they let you do it. You can do anything. Grab them by the pussy. You can do anything." The reaction from the American public was to elect him president less than a month later and excuse his remarks as simple "locker room talk."[61]

Perhaps the ugliest display of blame-the-victim rape culture occurred in the fall of 2018, just prior to the start of the confirmation hearings for Trump's nominee for the United States Supreme Court, Brett Kavanaugh. Reports surfaced that a Dr. Christine Blasey Ford, a professor of psychology at Palo Alto University and research psychologist at the Stanford University School of Medicine, had accused Kavanaugh of sexual assault during a Maryland house party when the pair were both teenagers in 1982. This set up a showdown and dueling testimony in front of the Senate, in which Blasey Ford tearfully and fearfully recounted her memories of being assaulted that day by an inebriated teenage Kavanaugh, while Kavanaugh denied every allegation. It was painful watching Blasey Ford on television, clearly on public trial to defend her truth, only to be interrogated about what and how much she drank that day, her prior sexual partners, and whether she had political motivations to sabotage

---

61 "US Election: Full Transcript of Donald Trump's Obscene Videotape," *BBC*, October 9, 2016, https://www.bbc.com/news/election-us-2016-37595321

Kavanaugh's Supreme Court chances. Kavanaugh, who came off angry and annoyed at the audacity of even being questioned on the topic, spent the day yelling at the people whose job it is to question the character of potential justices who serve for life. Kavanaugh's nomination was eventually approved, and he now sits on the Supreme Court. Meanwhile, Blasey Ford's life has been upended by the ordeal, requiring her to move residences and engage months of security detail to protect herself from the people angry at her for simply speaking up against her alleged assailant.[62]

According to statistics from the National Sexual Violence Resource Center, one in five women will be raped during their lifetimes. Just as troubling is the fact that 63 percent of sexual assaults—with both men and women victims—are not reported to police.[63] And when you look at the troubling cases of women accusing powerful men of sexual impropriety, it's not difficult to understand why so many victims choose not to come forward with their stories when the pattern is for society to blame and punish them.

Are there instances of women who lie about being sexually assaulted? Yes. But while we should always maintain the standard of innocent until proven guilty, that doesn't mean we should demonize accusers from the outset. If your first instinct is to ask a victim what they were wearing or why they were wherever they were when they were raped, as if their wardrobe or geographic

---

62 Bridget Read, "Christine Blasey Ford Speaks About Personal Security Costs Post-Kavanaugh Hearing, Pledges Leftover Donations to Survivors," *Vogue*, November 27, 2018, https://www.vogue.com/article/christine-blasey-ford-go-fund-me-donations-trauma-survivors?verso=true

63 "Statistics About Sexual Violence," *National Sexual Violence Resource Center*, accessed September 15, 2019, https://www.nsvrc.org/sites/default/files/publications_nsvrc_factsheet_media-packet_statistics-about-sexual-violence_0.pdf

location were in any way their fault, then you should dig a little deeper to ponder why you've not asked the perpetrator instead why they decided to rape and commit a crime.

This is rape culture—not just the reprehensible behavior of presidents, but the attitudes that everyday people hold that can reflect back onto your kids.

So, how can parents of boys combat this deeply engrained rape culture? For starters, it can begin with educating them about the concept of consent—something far more complex and nuanced than most parents convey to their sons. As I'm writing these words, I'm dealing with my oldest son having his first girlfriend. We've always been a family who talks about everything out in the open and without shame—correct anatomical names for body parts, homosexuality, the basics of sex, where babies come from, etc.—but it's different when it goes from an abstract idea to an actual person with a name and a face and a personality. Things got very real very quickly, and suddenly I felt I had so much to share with Will and absolutely no time to do it all because there he was, entering middle school, with a girlfriend. Granted, as far as I can tell, having a girlfriend at this age mostly means awkward Instagram posts and being embarrassed when your friends bring it up while hardly ever seeing in the other person, but still—my kid is dating!

That begged the question: where do I start? As a father, this is a seminal moment, and I knew that how I handled it would set the foundation for all our future discussions on the topic. While I knew I couldn't just make him drink from the fire hose when it comes to dating advice, I also felt that there was just so much he needed to know. So one night, just before bed, I asked Will if I could talk to him because I thought it was important that we have a chat now that he's a big shot with a girlfriend. As I sat on the edge of his bed, he wore the same look on his face that I did when I knew my parents were about to have "The Talk" with me. It was equal parts awkwardness, anxiety, and revulsion.

Thoughts of that talk from twenty-five years ago raced through my head as I searched for just the right words and approach to be effective with Will. My dad was (and still is) a wonderful father who imparted many important lessons, which led to me being a (mostly) good person, but I have to admit that his lessons on relationships were a little lacking. One of his messages stuck with me in particular. It was about consent: "Don't do anything with a girl unless she says yes first." Surely that's a good message, if a tad simplistic. Heterosexual men should absolutely not engage in any sexual activity with a woman if she hasn't given her consent, right? Except my still-forming teenage brain took that to mean: "As long as she says yes, we're good." And it took me more than a decade to realize that's a problem. First of all, it sets men up as the automatic initiators and women as the gatekeepers, and it ignores the fact that women can initiate and that men, too, do not automatically consent every time.

Second, it created an unhealthy mindset in me: I spent my later teens and college years doing everything possible to "get to yes" with girls. I knew I couldn't do anything without consent, because that meant it would be rape. But you don't have to rape someone to contribute to rape culture, and I absolutely did exactly that in my quest for yes. If I was dating a girl who was on the fence about having sex, I did everything I could to persuade her to consent. I'd buy her flowers, write her poems, and use those nice gestures as proof that I deserved sex. I begged, I pleaded, I cajoled, I manipulated, and I guilted my way to yes with more of my girlfriends than I care to admit, without ever realizing how problematic my actions were at the time. I was so used to the men I'd see on TV and the men I knew in my social circles who would talk about all the things they were doing to get girls to "put out" that I just assumed that was how it was done and conformed to the hive mentality without examining my actions. It wasn't until shortly after MJ and I were dating that I overheard her talking with some girlfriends about the pathetic guys in their lives who begged for sex—these men were so annoying and persistent in their pursuits that the women finally just gave in and slept with them just to get these guys off their backs. I remember breaking in to that conversation to ask how often that happened, and each and every one of them said it was entirely commonplace.

It stunned me for several reasons. First of all, I realized I was that guy. I was the obnoxious clown begging and angling for sex at every turn, the pathetically sad man they were referring to at that very moment. Secondly, it dawned on me that women were having sex not because they really wanted to, but because they had decided it was easier to do that than to deal with persistent nagging from guys like me. I vividly recall feeling, in that moment, how sad the situation was and how utterly clueless and stupid I had been. Because every time I had to negotiate with a woman to say yes, I celebrated in my head, and what I had been celebrating was actually a woman I had worn down to the point of her half-heartedly agreeing to have sex just so I'd shut up. It never dawned on me that consent shouldn't be the only goal. I was missing enthusiasm and eagerness. I had been looking solely for permission instead of making myself the type of person with whom women actually wanted to have sex with, freely and without reservation.

All this time I had fancied myself a good guy, simply because I had never raped anyone. As if not raping someone is a bragging point or badge of honor for men! That's how low we have stooped. And the entire time, I had been contributing to toxic masculinity by not understanding the complexities of consent and how men constantly put women in no-win positions that breed negativity and resentment. And I wondered why my relationships never went anywhere, and why sex had always been about conquests and tally marks as opposed to caring about the experience of the other person. Let me tell you, it is beyond jarring to realize you're a central part of the problem you always thought you were fighting against. Even though it was embarrassingly late in my life when I realized all this, it's now my mission to impart these lessons as early as possible to my boys so they're not as humiliatingly behind the curve as I was.

So, with all those thoughts swirling in my head as I perched on the edge of my oldest son's bed, my mind raced to find a way to convey that to him in a manner an eleven-year-old could comprehend. The conversation didn't begin so well as I stumbled around to find the words, and his cocked head and raised eyebrows told me I was failing to land my main points. He started to lose interest and began playing with our Maine Coon out of boredom. As I tried to forge on, the cat grew increasingly uncomfortable and tried to jump off the bed, but Will held it there because he loves Bruno's soft fur.

Then the lightbulb went off.

"Will, the cat doesn't want you to pet it right now. Are you noticing his body language? The fact that he's trying to get away? The meowing that lets you know he's unhappy? He's staying there for now because he loves you and doesn't want to hurt you, but he's clearly giving you multiple signs that he'd rather be somewhere else at the moment, and you're ignoring those signs. You're being selfish and you're not respecting the cat, who is clearly conveying that he wants to leave. Do you think it's right that just because you're bigger and stronger than he is that you get to decide what he does and where he can go? Buddy, this is what consent is. Think about if the cat were your girlfriend right now."

The look on his face told me everything I needed to know. It had landed.

"Oh," he said thoughtfully, his eyes going wide. "*Oh wow*! I totally get what you're saying now. That actually makes a lot of sense."

The irony here is that I hate cats. Detest them in a very primal way, actually. I've been trying to make my house cat-free for as long as I've been dating MJ, and this particular cat used to crap in my shoes (only my shoes, never anyone else's). It served as my personal nemesis. But that night, he was exactly what I needed to teach my kid a very important lesson I personally didn't learn until I was in my twenties.

The lesson about consent that I hope to impart to the parents reading this book is to talk to your kids about it early, often, and completely. Every kid is different, and you know your kids best, but I urge you not to put it off too long. If you do, you risk ending up with a boy who hopefully knows not to rape but who also has no clue he's contributing to toxic and harmful behavior that doesn't benefit him, women, or society in general. More than that, you're sentencing him to a sex life that consists of keeping score instead of scoring a point for the fulfillment of both parties. Besides, there's no reason enthusiastic consent shouldn't be sexy and wonderful. After all, if the other person says yes, then that's terrific!

Not letting your boys succumb to rape culture doesn't just end with a conversation about consent. It's also about being cognizant of the movies they watch, the music they listen to, and the video games they're playing. It's about telling them, in no uncertain terms, that "locker room talk" should *never* include kissing women against their will, grabbing their genitalia, and joking about sexual assault. It's about showing them the Brock Turners of the world and how wrong it is for the media narrative to focus on the loss of his swimming scholarship at Stanford instead of how he had raped an unconscious woman, and it's about how wrong it is for Turner's father to claim his son shouldn't go to prison just for "twenty minutes of action," when that action was rape.[64]

Rape culture is the normalization of violence against women as reflected in our cultural norms. It's the glamorization of sexual violence against women in pop culture; it is the dehumanization of women in the media. Rape culture lives on today, not just in our politics but also among our children—in the playground, at the dinner table with their parents, in front of the TV. Luckily, there is a solution. Our boys need to be brought up from a young age to respect women. To believe them. To be their allies at school and eventually at work. I tell my boys it is not enough for them to simply be men who don't mistreat women; they should strive to be men who also advocate for women. Who stand beside women even when it doesn't directly and personally benefit them in any way. And to recognize the rape culture in which we live and fight against from the inside, because women aren't going to fix this alone and this is truly a shared fight. This garbage only ends when men make a serious effort to get involved and be allies. That's a message we need to instill in our boys as early as possible.

PARENTING TIP #30: The problem with porn and hookup culture

I saw my first *Playboy* when I was still in grade school. Another boy had smuggled it into the Protestant church I was forced to attend as a young kid. He showed me the centerfold in the church

---

64 Elle Hunt, "20 minutes of action: father defends Stanford student son convicted of sexual assault," The Guardian, June 5, 2016, https://www.theguardian.com/us-news/2016/jun/06/father-stanford-university-student-brock-turner-sexual-assault-statement

basement where we usually hung out to skip Sunday School. A few years later when I was in the eighth or ninth grade, my dad showed me what he thought was my first *Playboy* during an entirely uncomfortable rite-of-passage-moment, which resulted in me pretending that I hadn't already combed through stacks of those magazines and memorized each Playmate of the Month. That was also the year I discovered softcore porn on Cinemax (or, as we called it, Skin-emax) and spent far too many hours sneaking downstairs during sleepovers at my house to watch poorly acted skin flicks with my friends.

Today, those days in the nineties are thought of as wholesome, nostalgic moments, because now, there's Pornhub.

Instead of the rare instances in my youth when I could actually get my hands on a VHS porn cassette, Pornhub has been providing free, unadulterated porn clips to anyone with an internet connection since 2007. The widespread availability of just about every kind of porn you could ever imagine, all searchable in different categories, makes imparting a realistic view of sex to our boys very difficult. A December 2018 *Esquire* article by Sarah Rense found that in 2018, people made a grand total of 33.5 billion visits to Pornhub, representing 92 million daily average visits to the site and nearly 4.8 million pornographic videos uploaded—enough hours for a single person to continuously watch porn without breaks for more than a century."[65] So, little Johnny, who you think is an angel and who you're sure would never watch smut? He's watching. He's watching a lot of it.

If you need proof, Peggy Orenstein's book *Boys & Sex* has it—in all its brutal honesty. She interviewed more than a hundred

---

65 Sarah Rense, "The Human Race Really Outdid Itself with Porn Searches in 2018," *Esquire*, December 12, 2018, https://www.esquire.com/lifestyle/sex/news/a52061/most-popular-porn-searches/

boys between the ages of sixteen and twenty-two who are either college-bound or in college, and most of them use Pornhub constantly. When they wake up in the morning, Pornhub. If they have ten minutes to spare in between classes, Pornhub. One college junior she interviewed said it's so reflexive he'll often find himself calling up Pornhub on his phone when he meant to check the weather or the news. A college sophomore in the book said Pornhub's launch coincided with him hitting puberty, which meant everything he learned about sex and masturbation was tied directly to Pornhub.[66] Boy after boy in her book admitted to watching untold hours of porn, many of them progressing from innocent searches to more hardcore pornography until they were viewing things such as women defecating in hotdog buns.

As absurd as it sounds, this is the baseline expectation for many, many men when it comes to how their sexual experiences should unfold. One survey of 2,500 college students found that 60 percent of respondents use porn to learn crucial information about sex.[67] With Orenstein's research of talking with boys, which directly backs up that sobering statistic, the fact of the matter is that Pornhub is acting as a sex educator for a majority of young kids, simply because their parents are uncomfortable with having the birds and the bees talk. As a parent, that should scare you. Actually, that should *terrify* you to your core. Because even if you tell boys to respect women and get consent, what they're hearing from you and what they're seeing on the internet are two very different (and conflicting) things.

---

66 Peggy Orenstein, "Boys & Sex: Young men on Hookups, Love, Porn, Consent, and Navigating the New Masculinity," Harper, 2020.

67 Abby Young-Powell, "Students Turn to Porn for Sex Education," *The Guardian*, Jan. 29, 2015, https://www.theguardian.com/education/2015/jan/29/students-turn-to-porn-for-sex-education

While there is certainly feminist porn and ethical porn being made, that is generally not the kind of porn most kids are watching on Pornhub and across the internet. I went to Pornhub.com, and here were the videos that popped up just from going to the homepage: "Therapist Cures Your Anxiety," "Fucking My Auntie's Face As My Stepuncle Walks in And Catches Us," "Petite College Freshman Moans Daddy While Fucked Doggy," and "No Mercy Anal Compilation—Tight Teens | Relentless Rough Fucking | Painal." The common theme in all of these videos is well-endowed men treating women like blow-up dolls with pulses, their fake and unconvincing moans silenced when men haphazardly jam their veiny third legs down their throats. Absurd? Yes. To be fair, even seventy-five percent of those 2,500 college students surveyed cited unrealistic expectations in the porn they watch. But, and this is the key, they're watching it anyway and internalizing what they see, because in the absence of proper sex education and honest conversations with parents, Pornhub fills the void.

So, what are kids internalizing when they watch porn? Orenstein's book finds that while heterosexual males who watch porn are more likely to be accepting of same-sex marriage, they're less likely to support affirmative action for women and to only tepidly endorse gender equality as it relates to work, politics, and life. Also, college students who regularly consume porn are more likely to consider what's being portrayed as real, become sexually active sooner, have more partners, have higher rates of pregnancy, and experience more sexual aggression. And if you stop and think about it, it makes total sense. When watching porn, boys are bombarded by images that tell them they have to have ridiculously gargantuan penises and stamina that lasts for hours, and that women exist in the sexual realm solely as props to please them. The default in most heterosexual porn is rough sex that includes forcing a woman's head down to gag on an erect penis or rough sex (often anal) that takes place without a condom and with little to no communication between partners.

Look, I'm not going to go all anti-porn on you (I still watch porn occasionally, and sometimes with my wife on the rare occasion that we have the house to ourselves). Curiosity about sex is natural and to be encouraged, and I think some kinds of porn when consumed responsibly and in moderation are generally okay, provided that parents properly communicate with boys the realities of sex, outside of the porn industry. The latter is what's missing most of the time because parents aren't letting kids know that most of what they see in porn is not normal, healthy, or realistic. It's why we have a generation of confused boys who grow into men who are shocked when they try to get intimate with women for the first time and find that those women don't appreciate any of the nonsense they've seen acted out their whole lives. It also leads to boys assuming this rough and non-communicative sex is what women want, which has a higher likelihood of ending in sexual assault if boys are forcing a woman's head down to their crotch without asking.

Parents, don't assume your boys know not to do that. Orenstein's book has some devastating examples of nice guys engaging in extraordinarily problematic sexual acts with girls without the slightest recognition of a problem. Even outside of porn, hook-up culture for many teens is all about status and the number of partners you can get up to, and too many boys are only thinking of how to get that number higher so they can gain credibility with their (usually male) peers. Is she into it? Is she enjoying herself? Did she say she liked it? These are not questions boys are taught to ask—either by watching porn or from talks with their parents.

Sure, if they step back and gain some perspective, they're usually able to see the problem. But if no one has told them otherwise and they're inundated by a deluge of porn telling them women love it when guys absentmindedly orgasm all over their faces? Well, is it any wonder why the #MeToo movement exists and why there are so many stories about sexual assault?

Boys are taking what they learn from porn and applying it in the real world despite there not being much reality in those videos whatsoever. That mindset not only has negative repercussions in the bedroom, it also further perpetuates the stereotype of women being seen merely as holes to be plugged and unimportant props that exist solely for the benefit of men. This impacts how boys view and treat girls outside of the context of sex as well. Not to mention the damage this does to girls. Girls who watch porn and think they need to take an inherently passive role and be sexually demeaned in order to keep men happy are also put at a devastating disadvantage; after all, porn teaches them to prioritize a man's needs and desires above their own.

I was going to wait to talk to my son about porn, but after reading Orenstein's book, I changed my mind and spoke with him immediately. It was awkward, no ifs, ands, or buts about it. But it was also extremely necessary, because as it turns out, at just eleven years old, he was already past due for that chat. And while I'm certainly not going to tell him to watch porn or send him a selection of my favorites, I'm also not going to pretend it doesn't exist or harbor any delusions that he's not going to watch it. Despite all the filters and safeguards I have on his phone and our computers, kids will find a way. They always have and always will. Just like I don't believe abstinence is a realistic solution to teen pregnancy, I also know that shouting, "NO PORN!" isn't going to work, either. I'm explaining to him that these are actors engaging in fantasy, and that even though they're paid most of the time, most of them are not making much and are sometimes doing it in dangerous conditions. I'm telling him in no uncertain terms that porn is fake and that when he does eventually find himself in a sexual situation with a girl (he's identified himself as heterosexual), he doesn't have to guess at what she likes—he should just ask her and find out straight from the source. I also urge parents to check out amaze.org, which has content that, as they market it, "takes the awkward out of sex ed" by sticking to the "More Info. Less Weird." mantra.

As one of Orenstein's subjects says, kids *want* their parents to talk to them about sex and porn. They might cringe, but boys are not only looking for that information, they're looking to their fathers for personal advice and anecdotes. They want to hear about what works, what's healthy, and what they found regrettable. Yes, that's going to be *super* uncomfortable, and it might feel like a root canal is a preferable way to spend the hour, but it's worth it. I promise.

If you take anything away from this book, I hope it's remembering that if you don't talk to your boys about porn and sex, then Pornhub and the internet will be their default sex-ed instructor. And as we've seen, that's unacceptable.

PARENTING TIP #31: Don't fear the #MeToo movement; learn from it

The #MeToo movement, which has held many high-profile men accountable for rape and sexual assault during the past few years, is often erroneously seen as an attack on men. While some men have looked inward and taken note of the fact that one in three women experience sexual violence while nearly one in five women experience completed or attempted rape during their life-times at the hands of men,[68] others have dismissed #MeToo as nothing more than gender propaganda fueled by social justice warriors. Instead of listening to victim accounts and engaging in self-reflection to see how their past actions may have contrib-uted to the toxic culture that dismisses victims while protecting perpetrators, their only actions have been doubling down on the angst aimed at women and engaging in acts of self-preservation.

For instance, there is a belief among many evangelical men called the "Billy Graham Rule," named after the famed preacher, where men of faith decide not to spend any time alone with women who are not their wives. The original idea is to limit the tempta-tion to be unfaithful, but lately, this line of thinking has come into vogue again for slightly different reasons. Today, we have named it the "Mike Pence Rule" because Vice President Pence refuses to be alone with anyone other than "Mother" (which is the not-at-all creepy way he references his wife). Likewise, Mississippi guber-natorial candidate Robert Foster made headlines in the summer of 2019 for invoking the Billy Graham Rule when he denied a female journalist the opportunity to shadow him for a day on the campaign trail unless she brought another male colleague with her. While many people saw this as outright discrimination against a professional female journalist simply trying to do her job—a job Foster allows men to do with no problems—Foster maintained his actions protect him not only against any potential infidelity, but also against the current #MeToo movement and any allegations of impropriety from women.

The problem here is indicative of preexisting gender bias being taken to an extreme and going sideways. The desire to remain loyal

---

68 "Preventing Sexual Violence," *Centers for Disease Control*, 2019, https://www.cdc.gov/violenceprevention/pdf/SV-Factsheet.pdf

to one's partner is a good one at its core, but it's bullshit when it gets to the point of disallowing yourself or your spouse to ever interact on a one-on-one basis with a member of the opposite sex. I have female friends and my wife has male friends. Sometimes we hang out with those friends alone. Why? *Because I trust my wife, and she trusts me.* Honestly, if you're in a marriage that can't withstand a solo dinner with a colleague or a catch-up with a friend who happens to be of the opposite sex, then that marriage is already in extraordinarily peril. What a horrible message we'd be sending to our boys as parents if they hear one parent tell the other that they're "not allowed" to hang out with a friend of the opposite sex because of distrust and fragile egos. Again, as we've discussed, this assumes men are untamed animals who operate solely by their id and can't be trusted without fear of whipping out their erections, while women are all just jezebels out to steal a man. It also flies in the face of the mutual trust and commitment that should be the foundation of a marriage. It shouldn't take a sexist rule to ensure fidelity in a marriage, and frankly, it's a form of abusive control to forbid your spouse from hanging out with a friend just because you're not secure.

Unfortunately, Pence and Foster are hardly the only men adopting this antiquated mindset, and it isn't just a problem in the home. According to a 2019 survey from LeanIn.org, 60 percent of male managers in America are uncomfortable participating in a common work activity with a woman, such as mentoring, working alone, or socializing together.[69] That represents a 32 percent increase from just one year ago. Men who hold senior positions are twelve times more likely to avoid one-on-one meetings with female junior colleagues, nine times more likely to hesitate to

---

69 "Men, Commit To Mentor Women," *LeanIn.org*, accessed September 15, 2019, https://leanin.org/mentor-her

travel together for work, and six times more likely to hesitate to go to work dinners with women as opposed to male coworkers. Why is this phenomenon suddenly occurring? 36 percent of American men surveyed reported being uncomfortable with how it would look being alone with a female coworker. Today, the Billy Graham Rule is occurring in workplaces all over America, and it is extraordinarily damaging to everyone.

For example, I'm overweight, but I know the answer to my obesity is not locking myself away in solitary confinement and avoiding all foods forever. The solution is to learn how to make more informed nutritional decisions so I can be healthier. One of my sons used to be completely petrified of elevators, but while avoiding them and taking the stairs might do wonders for his cardio, it's not a realistic solution for him to avoid elevators for all of eternity. So, we taught him how elevators work and gave him the confidence to eventually use them with less and less unease every time.

So, it stands to reason that the solution for men at work who are wary of spending time with women colleagues—because they don't want to be "#MeToo"-ed or accused of anything untoward—isn't to lock themselves away and ignore half the population. It's simply to—wait for it—not sexually harass their female coworkers!

Another example of fairly routine preexisting gender biases turning into something harmful is the Men's Rights Activist (MRA) movement. For the blessedly uninitiated, MRAs are a group of wildly off-kilter gentlemen who believe it isn't women, but rather men, who are discriminated against in society, namely because men are obligated to sign up for the military draft at eighteen, men work the majority of backbreaking industrial and manufacturing jobs, men are victims of domestic abuse at the hands of women, and men primarily get screwed over in divorces involving custody battles and alimony. The thing is, they're not totally wrong about the last two points, which is what makes the vitriol and hate so frustrating and disturbing. MRAs have some legitimate points, but those points get lost in an avalanche of anti-feminist, anti-equality, and often violently misogynistic fury that negates any and all sense they had in the first place, such as their belief that feminist women gatekeep their vaginas unfairly. For MRAs, everything that doesn't go right in their lives is the fault of women.

I've run into these guys on social media a few times, and their mindset is terrifying. It's all alpha male, anti-woman nonsense fueled by anger and entitlement. They are known to go after prominent feminists online with unbelievably degrading insults and even violent rape fantasies, as described in Katie J. M. Baker's 2013 *Jezebel* piece titled "Rape and Death Threats: What Men's Rights Activists Really Look Like." In that piece, Baker describes how a feminist named Charlotte who protested at an MRA speech paid the price via online harassment after the fact. "They've circulated her personal info, dredged up details about her past (one fellow told Charlotte that her dog who died years ago would be 'disappointed' in her), and sent her messages threatening to rape and kill and rape her again—one of the more PG-rated ones promises that 'we will not rest until your unholy blood is shed.'"[70] This male ugliness came out again in full force during the 2016 election as the nation faced the very real possibility of its first female president in Hillary Clinton, and I'll go to my grave believing that it helped fuel a misogynist's rise to the office in Donald Trump.

---

70 Katie J.M. Baker, "Rape and Death Threats: What Men's Rights Activists Really Look Like," *Jezebel*, April 22, 2013, https://jezebel.com/rape-and-death-threats-what-mens-rights-activists-rea-476882099

The irony in all of this is that MRAs claim they do what they do to lower suicide rates among men, create more fairness in the family court system, and generally advocate more for boys and men. But in reality, I believe they're simply looking to silence women by strengthening the negative societal forces that brought us the patriarchy in the first place. MRAs, Billy Graham rule enthusiasts, incels—these groups didn't just magically appear out of the ether. They are the inevitable outcome of gender biases that take hold when our young boys are subject to things like pornography that degrades women, media messaging that reinforces patriarchal values, and failure of parents to talk with boys about gender bias and toxic masculinity.

Our boys need to know that you don't build yourself up by tearing other people down, and that this amount of anger, resentment, and violence isn't going to help anyone. If your version of "helping" involves name-calling and wishing someone gets raped or has a cock put in their mouth to shut her up, you're on the wrong side of the fence. Unfortunately, changing an adult male MRA's mind is a Herculean if not impossible task, so it's incumbent on parents to give boys the foundation they need when they're still young to value equality of all kinds. Teach boys that women don't owe them anything as far as sex is concerned, and that while unfairness and bias does exist for us all, the simple fact is it's much more advantageous to be a white, straight male in America than it is to be a woman (or a person of color or a member of the LGBTQ+, etc.). And once your children are equipped with this knowledge, teach them to advance society in such a way where there will be more understanding, more dialogue, and more acceptance.

The answer isn't taking on an Us vs. Them mentality, isolation, or fear of repercussions; it's even more integration, communication, and self-education. It's not that difficult to be a good and respectful human being. I don't care whether it's women, gay people, people of color, or trans folks—my boys need more interaction with a wider variety of people, not less. I want them to know that an incalculable amount of knowledge can learned by engaging with other people who don't look like they do. I also want their relationships to be based on trust, not fear. The Billy Graham Rule only serves to further divide us and throw up walls, and holy shit do we have enough talk of walls lately.

PARENTING TIP #32: Don't spank your kids

I wasn't spanked often growing up, and I was never hit with a belt or a switch. But, like most kids I knew, the threat always loomed. If I was spanked, it only happened when I was little, for fighting with my brother, trying to run into the street, and one time for swearing. As a kid, being spanked by my parents felt like I was getting into the ring with Mike Tyson, but in reality, it was simply a swat on the backside that hurt more emotionally than physically. So, when I became a parent, I took spanking and put it in my toolbox of parenting techniques to use when necessary, since "I was spanked and I turned out fine."

With my oldest son, it worked. I can count on one hand the number of times we had to spank him, and each time we did, it had the desired effect. Once, as a toddler, he was standing in the dog's water bowl and trying to pry the protective covers off the electrical outlet. When I looked up, fears of electrocution flooded my mind as I rushed over to yank him out and then popped him on the butt before I could even think about it because I was so scared. He never did it again, and I continued to look at spanking as an effective weapon in my arsenal of parenting techniques.

I recounted that story in an online parenting group I was part of at the time and was surprised by the disapproving responses. Then, other parents started linking to peer-reviewed research that showed, in no uncertain terms, that spanking was unequivocally bad for kids.

According to a piece by the American Psychological Association (APA) in 2012, "many studies have shown that physical punishment—including spanking, hitting, and other means of causing pain—can lead to increased aggression, antisocial behavior, physical injury, and mental health problems for children." In the piece, Alan Kazdin, PhD, a director of the Child Conduct Clinic at the Yale University Parenting Center, said, "Spanking doesn't work. You cannot punish out these behaviors that you do not want. There is no need for corporal punishment based on the research. We are not giving up an effective technique. We are saying this is a horrible thing that does not work."[71] In the same article, Sandra Graham-Bermann, PhD, psychology professor and principal investigator for the Child Violence and Trauma Laboratory at the University of Michigan, said that while physical punishment can work at temporarily stopping problematic behavior via instilling fear in the child of being hit in the moment, it doesn't carry into the long-term. And in many cases, it makes kids even more aggressive. Furthermore, the United Nations Committee on the Human Rights of the Child issued a directive in 2006 calling physical punishment "legalized violence against children" that should be eliminated in all settings.[72]

---

71 Brendan Smith, "The Case Against Spanking," *American Psychological Association* Vol. 43 No. 4 (April 2012): 60.

72 United Nations Convention on the Rights of a Child, 2006, https://www.ohchr.org/en/professionalinterest/pages/crc.aspx

I read these studies, and I saw these recommendations, and I heard the experts extolling the virtues of finding other punishments outside of spanking. Yet I refused to eliminate it from my child discipline repertoire because 1) I truly didn't think it was harmful; 2) I thought kids who aren't spanked get spoiled and bratty; and 3) it worked with Will, so what did these "experts" really know?

Then came Sam, our second child.

Sam misbehaved from the get-go. Classic middle child. He had none of my oldest son's composed and contemplative nature, but he made up for that in curiosity, impetuousness, and temper. Sam did everything he wasn't supposed to, and we tried everything we normally would have before going to the extreme step of spanking—redirection, positive reinforcement, distraction, bribery, timeouts; you name it, we tried it. But nothing worked. One day, after Sam repeatedly pulled our dog's fur, grabbed his paws, and tried to ride him for the thousandth time, I warned him that if he didn't stop, he was going to be spanked. When he kept going, I followed through on my threat. I'll never forget, until the day I die, what happened next. He looked at me, wide-eyed in surprise, without a hint of fear, and said, "No hurt!" Then he went right back to torturing the dog, but this time with more gusto. As time went on, I mistakenly thought that I just needed to be firmer and escalate the situation. I threatened to smack his butt harder until it did hurt, except he was digging in as well and acting out even worse than before. If anything, I realized that the spanking just made him more aggressive and entrenched. With Will, it was one spank and he was good, but Sam? Sam was an entirely different beast. That was the first time I learned what should have been an obvious lesson—that you can't parent your kids the same way because they're all different.

When I noticed Sam trying to spank his brothers and some-times his friends soon after, I realized his default responses to stimuli were all turning physical and rough. Then came the ADHD and ODD diagnoses and a laundry list of questions from doctors about how we were raising him and, yes, whether or not we spanked him. I sheepishly answered in the affirmative and proceeded to get lectured on why that's not a good idea. Of course, I already knew the reasons why—because I had read and ignored them based on my own upbringing and the toxic mascu-linity bullshit I was still buying into, even though I always tried so hard to overcome it. I had been duped into believing I wasn't a real dad unless I smacked my kid around to stop him from becoming a spoiled brat.

Thinking about how ridiculous my actions were still brings a tear to my eye. There I was, fully aware that boys are thrown into a world of physical brutality and aggression, and somehow I thought adding to that via spanking was different. Better. That it would magically be exempt from all the other forms of violence young boys are exposed to. Sam is proof that aggression breeds aggression and that kids don't benefit when the people they're supposed to trust most in the world choose to hit them. I naively thought that if I smacked him on the butt with an open hand and not on the face or body with a closed fist, I was okay and not part of the prob-lem. When I take a step back to really think about that "logic" for a second, it boggles my mind. Yet I know full well I'm not alone and that millions of well-meaning parents think nothing of spank-ing their kid and even consider it responsible parenting.

Here's the real test. If you walk out of your house and whack the first person you see on the street on the ass, what do you think will happen? Spoiler alert—the police will be called and you will likely be arrested for assault, even if that person was being loud and obnoxious. It doesn't matter—you hit someone, you pay the price. If smacking a stranger is a criminal offense, why the hell is smacking your kid any different? The answer is it's not.

In a world that sees our boys resort to violence as a default setting for just about everything, spanking unnecessarily adds to the stew of toxic masculinity in a way I don't want to be a part of anymore. We've never spanked our youngest, and I'll never spank any of my kids again. I actually went up to each of my two oldest sons to apologize—I told them that I had been wrong and that it would never happen again. Men are not infallible, nor should their authority be beyond reproach. If you've wronged someone, you need to own up and apologize, and I hope to model that behavior for my kids.

I won't sit here and tell you I've found the answer to my child discipline problems, because I haven't. I try reward charts, time-outs, physical labor, positive reinforcement, redirection, taking things away, and everything else every expert has recommended. Does it work? Sometimes. When it doesn't, I try something else. But I will no longer hit my kids, and I'm sorry I ever thought that was a good idea. If you're still a proponent of corporal punishment, I hope you reconsider. Your kids might still misbehave, but at least you won't be joining them in the process.

PARENTING TIP #33: The problem with chivalry

When I started frequenting feminist circles to expand my perspective on things, the topic of chivalry was a major roadblock and an embarrassing stumbling point for me.

Chivalry was originally a code by which medieval knights were supposed to conduct themselves gallantly, and, like a lot of men I know, I was raised to believe in it and apply it to my dating life. Open the car door, pull out her chair at dinner, *always* pay for said dinner, put your hand on her lower back as you introduce her into the room first, walk her to her door, hold open doors in public, and walk closest to the street when you're both walking side-by-side—these were the things I had been taught were non-negotiable. I never gave it a second thought, because why would I? They seemed like good things. Kind things. Noble things. Many men, myself included, are brought up to believe chivalry is as necessary as basic good manners, like "please" and "thank you." And why the hell would anyone possibly be against good manners?

I even went so far as to pen a truly unfortunate guest column in August 2011 at the *Good Men Project*, sticking up for chivalry and lambasting the people I saw as attacking good manners. Reading it now makes me cringe. Looking back on how little I knew and realizing how wrong I was is painful beyond words. I hate that my ignorant blathering still floats around on the internet, but that's part of my journey. To embrace it, here's a little snippet of my idiocy: "If the biggest problem you have with men is that they randomly hold open doors or help you carry heavy groceries to your car, I really don't want to hear it. In the words of Jack Nicholson in *A Few Good Men*, 'I'd rather you just say thank you and go on your way.' . . . As someone who routinely holds open doors and gives up his seat on subways to women (and some men) without any expectations whatsoever, I have to request we put a stop to this idiocy. Common courtesy is a good thing. Manners are a good thing. Let's keep it that way."[73]

---

73 Aaron Gouveia, "Damned If We Do, Damned If We Don't," The Good Men Project, August 3, 2011, https://goodmenproject.com/ethics-values/damned-if-we-do-damned-if-we-dont/

I was soon taken to task for those views. At first, it was really hard to hear the criticisms, and frankly, I was confused as I truly had no understanding of how anyone could be against chivalrous actions. But after poring over response after response, largely saying the same things, I knew where I had gone wrong.

The problem with chivalry is rooted in the topic of "gendered civility"—that the chivalrous person is being polite solely and specifically to women, and usually because they hope to gain something from the transaction. The people who had commented on my article pointed out that many women do feel infantilized at the automatic assumption that they need men to walk them to their cars or pull open doors for them, as if they lack the strength or agency. They also pointed out that I was foisting my own patriarchal values on them, even if they didn't want or ask for chivalry. Finally, the knockout blow came when someone in an online discussion asked me if I fancied myself a gentleman, to which I answered yes, and then she proceeded to ask me how it was gentlemanly to forbid a woman from paying for a dinner or opening her own door even if she expressed her desire to do so. Chivalry, if unwelcome, completely ignores a woman's perspective and wishes.

At the end of the day, I explain to my boys that all we're really talking about here is kindness and civility—the sex of the recipient shouldn't be an issue at all. Holding a door open for someone is still a good thing, as long as I'm holding it open for any man, woman, or child and not doing it based solely on the other person's gender and my assumptions about what they need. Paying for dinner is usually appreciated, as long as the person I'm trying to treat is on board with it. And if someone is nervous about walking back to her car or back home late at night, ask if she'd like you to accompany her. If the answer is yes, great. If it is no, don't force your knightly code on her because all you're doing is taking away her agency, after she's told you that's not what she wants.

But make no mistake, I'm not advocating for a world without manners or kindnesses. And I'm certainly not saying that women want to do everything themselves or that they don't appreciate help. That's not the case at all. But as boys and men, we have to be aware if our chivalrous intentions come with an expectation of reciprocity, which may force women into a position that makes them uncomfortable. Some men may complain that they're damned if they do and damned if they don't—that was the title of my piece on the *Good Men Project* . . . so I'm talking about 2011 me—but those men haven't yet realized that they don't need to choose between being a gentleman and being an asshole. There's a whole lot of in-between to be found.

Parents need to remind boys that being nice is its own reward, and that niceness and kind gestures are not a reward card that ends with benefits if they get enough points. Raise kids to be considerate because that's the right way to act, not for a reward, especially if the reward is sex. Remember, boys need to hear they are not owed sex from women as much as possible, no matter how many dinner tabs they pick up, doors they open, or jackets they give up to keep another person warm. Gendered politeness is not really polite at all, and communication, as always, is key. If a woman really wants to pay for her own drink or meal, then teach boys to respect her wish just as they would if a person of the same sex asked to split the bill. When in doubt, kids can never go wrong listening to and respecting the wishes of other people, so try to make that the default setting for boys.

PARENTING TIP #34: Let boys know it's not all about the money

I have always struggled with my attitude toward money, as well as the concept I have that it is tied to my masculinity. It's been a deeply problematic issue to the point of negatively impacting my marriage, and just before writing this chapter, it popped up again, this time in my children.

Growing up, I always knew my dad was obsessed with money, mainly because he spent most of his childhood being raised by a single mom, and they didn't always have much. He always swore that when he had kids, he'd make damn sure that they wouldn't want for anything. For the most part, he delivered on that promise. When my parents had me in their early twenties, neither of them had a college degree. My mom managed a McDonald's when I was a baby, and my dad helped start a stainless-steel business that he still works at to this day as vice president. We lived in a ramshackle house for the first ten years of my life, and I barely remember seeing my dad because he was *always* at work, building a business with his partner from scratch. When he wasn't working, he was serving various roles as an elected and appointed official for our small Massachusetts town. Even from a very young age, I knew he was tortured by the knowledge that he was missing our childhood. He missed the moment I hit my first over-the-fence homerun in Little League, so we drove over to Town Hall where he was serving as a Selectman after the game, and I caught his attention mid-meeting and mouthed *homerun*, at which point he jumped out of his chair to come over and give me a tearful hug. He'd constantly apologize to us for not being around, but the reasons were there was a mortgage to pay, mouths to feed, and clothes to buy.

When we moved into a new, bigger house, my dad was so proud and happy. We had two-and-a-half bedrooms, and my brother and I no longer had to sleep in the same room. We had an actual shower, when before we'd only had a bath. I also remember that he bought a 50-inch big-screen TV to mark the occasion, and it was the very first thing to enter the new house (even before us). I knew that in his mind, he had made it. He had accomplished what every breadwinner strives for—a proper home for his family to grow up in. The only problem was a bigger house equaled a bigger mortgage payment, and my dad had to work even harder while my mom did her best Superwoman impression as the world's most involved stay-at-home parent.

I'll never forget the camping trip our family took when I was in high school and getting ready for college. My dad sat me down and had a talk with me that I wouldn't fully understand until much later in life. He opened up about all the stress he felt as a provider, all the plates he had to keep spinning in the air and the masters he had to serve. He tearfully spoke about the sacrifice men like him had to make and all the time he had missed watching us grow up in order to make sure we'd have the things we needed. And he jokingly lamented the fact that just as I was becoming interesting and fun to be around, I would soon be leaving for college. While Teenage Me couldn't fully grasp his message, Adult Me now understands his pain all too well and has felt those same moments of loss and helplessness.

When I first met MJ, I was working as a sales representative at my dad's business making peanuts; she, on the other hand, was a rock-star manager for Bank of America, and damn did she make bank! She was a top-performer in the top 1 percent of managers and earned trips to the Bahamas, as well as fat bonuses. Her salary was more than double mine—and that, ridiculously, was a problem for me.

My friends referred to MJ as my "sugar mama." The men in my life smiled and asked if I received an allowance from her. They openly questioned why someone as beautiful and successful as MJ would choose to be with me, especially since I wasn't bringing home a fat paycheck. On the outside, I rolled with the punches and embraced the teasing, jokingly referring to myself as a "kept man" and telling my friends who wanted to go out that I had to "check with the boss." Hell, I even managed to convince myself that I had become a progressive, modern man who was just fine with his wife making more money and being more successful than me. I performed a rousing "fake it till you make it" performance to convince myself and everyone around me that I was fine with the situation.

But when the recession hit in 2007 to 2008, MJ lost her job. Even though she got a new one, it wasn't at the same level. Then she got sick and couldn't work, and suddenly money was very much an issue. I was a newspaper reporter at the time, making even less money than I had been making as a sales rep, so I began looking for a new job. When I found one as a content manager for a company near Boston and discovered the salary would be double what I was making at the newspaper, my heart nearly leapt out of my chest. I was ecstatic. But my happiness wasn't an "oh my God we can finally start paying our bills on time and MJ won't have to go back to work so she can focus on getting healthier and we can survive as a family unit" type of happy. Instead, I felt a decided and intense emotion that screamed, *"Thank fucking God I finally make more money than my wife; I'm a real man now!"*

I hated that I felt that way, even in that moment. It was dick-ish, stupid, and completely backward. I feel shame just writing it down on these pages. But it's the truth, and I have to own it. I was feeling a primal, Neanderthal-level urge to unfurl my manhood on the table next to my paycheck. Even though I now hate the idea of a "Man Card," at that moment I wished someone had been there to give me mine. I felt like, at any moment, all of my male relatives, dead and alive, were going to come out of a room filled with cigar smoke, with firm handshakes and bourbon, while clapping me on the back and welcoming me to the club. All that posturing I had done telling people I was cool with a wife who out-earned me? Garbage. I had been lying to myself, and the second I made more money than her, I was relieved in a way that both perplexed and disturbed me.

I don't want this feeling to ever strike my boys. Or *any* boy. That kind of pressure is toxic, and it will ultimately manifest itself in a negative way. My wife is truly proud of me and all of my accomplishments, but she felt that way even when I was a thirty-two-year-old print journalist making $34,000 a year despite having a decade of experience. Meanwhile, even though I was proud of her and all her accomplishments, it wasn't pure or wholehearted. Despite putting on my best act, it's clear I was also very jealous of her success. When she was let go and had to take another banking job for less money, a part of me was actually happy, because I felt it got us a little closer to being even. Just think for a second how fucked up it is that a small part of me rejoiced even though my family had less money to stay afloat, simply because my fragile male ego couldn't take being out-earned by a woman. Not only is that anger-inducing, it's also pathetic. A partner who can't be happy for his significant other's success is a pretty shitty partner, and I've spent a lot of time since that realization trying to make it up to her.

Whoever my sons end up partnering with, I hope they fully support them without selfishness or shame. And whatever their financial state in life, I hope they feel proud of their successes without buying into the misconception that they have to earn enough money to be considered "a man." I urge them to not only value their partners, but also themselves, regardless of how much their take-home pay is at the end of every week.

But I also want my boys to know that in some respects, salary absolutely matters. Namely when it comes to the gender wage gap.

According to PayScale's report "The State of The Gender Pay Gap in 2019," the uncontrolled gender pay gap sees women making only $0.79 for every dollar men earn. But even when they examined the controlled gender pay gap—women and men with the same employment characteristics doing similar jobs—women still only earn $0.98 for every dollar earned by a man with the exact same qualifications.[74] Men's rights activists and misogynists everywhere will argue until the end of time that there is no gender wage gap and that women earn less because they take off big chunks of time to have kids, which is garbage reasoning. Women are paid less. End of story.

Never was that more glaring than during the 2019 World Cup, which saw the US Women's National Team win its fourth title since 1991. The men? They have had just one quarterfinal appearance and three trips to the Round of 16 in that same timespan. Despite their winning ways, a lawsuit filed by US women's players claims there were distinct differences related to the manner of compensation for the men as compared to the women for past performances at the World Cup. The women received $1.725 million for winning the 2015 event, according to the lawsuit, while the men received $5.375 million simply for reaching the Round of 16 in 2014. And while the women were galvanizing a nation and battling the best opposing players from around the

---

74 "The State of the Gender Pay Gap in 2019," *PayScale*, accessed September 15, 2019, https://www.payscale.com/data/gender-pay-gap

globe, in addition to fending off attacks from their own president, the men didn't even make the last World Cup held in Russia.

It's vital for parents to talk openly and honestly with their kids, especially boys, about the existence of pay inequality for men and women because, with any luck, it will motivate boys to join the fight for equality. It can't be stressed enough that women fighting these battles on their own is not ideal. Boys can and should know about these issues so they can grow up to become men who will help fight for equality in the workplace, at home, and in society in general—simply because it's the right and fair thing to do.

PARENTING TIP #35: Reexamine your religion when bringing up kids

We've tackled politics and guns, so why not complete the trifecta of controversy and move right on to religion?

I grew up a non-Catholic in a *very* Catholic town and went on to marry a Catholic woman, and for the life of me I'll never understand how so many wonderful people associate themselves with a religion that is clearly not intent on equality. Mary McAleese, former president of Ireland, said in a March 2018 *British Broadcasting Corporation* (BBC) article that the Catholic Church is one of the last great bastions of misogyny,[75] and you can't really argue with her on that point. Can women be priests? Nope. Are women told by the Catholic Church that they're going to hell for eternity if they maintain their own bodily autonomy and opt for an abortion? Yup. Does the Church look kindly on

---

75 "Catholic Church an 'Empire of Misogyny' – Mary McAleese," *BBC*, March 8, 2018, https://www.bbc.com/news/world-europe-43330026

women taking contraception in order to avoid getting pregnant? Not one bit.

It is perplexing to me to have Catholic friends and know Catholic people and be married to a woman who still considers herself Catholic—good, decent people—who fight for equality and against misogyny every single day; yet you also find them adhering to a religion that clearly views women as "other" and therefore lesser. And although they try to excuse it to me by claiming their specific church is progressive, the fact remains that only men are allowed to hold power in the Church as priests and bishops and cardinals and popes. Men dictate what women should and shouldn't do with their own bodies. And Catholic men spent decades covering for and enabling rampant sexual abuse by male clergy members—not only perpetrated on parishioners, but also nuns. It was only in 2019 that Pope Francis acknowledged the Catholic Church's "persistent problem of sexual abuse of nuns by priests and even bishops," according to a *New York Times* article by Jason Horowitz and Elizabeth Dias that was published on February 5.[76]

It's not just Catholicism, of course. Many fundamentalist Christian sects don't allow women to be ordained and evangelical Christian values like sexual purity and the submission of women to their husbands are considered sacrosanct. I guess that's what happens when you base a faith off a woman fucking it up for all of us by snacking on fruit that she was tricked into eating by a talking snake. And whether it's the Muslim faith (although widely misunderstood and exaggerated for political purposes by so many), which undoubtedly has issues with veiling, divorce

---

76 Jason Horowitz, Elizabeth Dias, "Pope Acknowledges Nuns Were Sexually Abused by Priests and Bishops," *New York Times*, February 5, 2019, https://www.nytimes.com/2019/02/05/world/europe/pope-nuns-sexual-abuse.html

laws, the young legal age for marriage, polygamy, and even honor killings in extreme instances, or the entrenched misogyny of orthodox Jewish people, the bottom line is that women aren't treated well by many religions—all while men are simultaneously and undeservedly exalted. I'd ask parents to take a step back and simply ask themselves if their religion is an acceptable model or belief system to bring kids up in if they want to teach them to become respectable, functional members of society.

As you might've already guessed, I'm a heathen atheist.

I didn't start off life that way. I'm the product of a Catholic father and a Protestant mother who was baptized and confirmed in a liberal Protestant Church after many years of Sunday School. Shit, I was even a church choir standout. In addition to my maternal grandmother being a member of the Boston Pops, Tanglewood, and a master concert pianist, she was also the church choir director. Which meant, whether I liked it or not, I was not only going to church every Sunday; I was also going to sing unto the Lord while there.

But it wasn't long until a confluence of events began to make me question my religion in general.

For starters, biblical literalists have always confused me, because even from a young age, I could tell these were just stories and allegorical tales meant to prove a point. Except it was clear that not everyone felt that way, and I quickly learned that questioning the Word of God went over like a fart in church. Ultimately, it was discovering how other religions shut down women and rejected members of the LGBTQ+ community that put the nail in my believer coffin. Well, that and my intense love of sports, which saw practices and games coincide with church. I can't tell you how many times I had a soccer or baseball or basketball uniform on under my choir robe, and I can still hear my grandmother scolding me for wearing cleats in church and ducking out early to get to my games.

I could also never get over the fact that so many people said they believed in a God who supposedly valued all human life as equal, but who would allow rampant discrimination and even hate to rule the day and the values of the Church. Even today, the official stance of the Catholic Church is that homosexuality is a sin and Pope Francis—by far the most liberal and progressive of popes—is against allowing women to enter the priesthood. I truly believe that you're not helping the case for equality if you subscribe to a faith that treats people differently based on sex or sexual orientation; and if you give money and time to that organization, you're enabling it. Even for those working to change the culture from the inside, I just can't square participating in something I know to be problematic.

Which is why one of the biggest fights my wife and I have ever had was about our kids and religion.

Although all of my kids have been to various church services, none of my children are baptized—a fact that deeply disturbs some members of my family. MJ wanted to baptize them as babies, and I vehemently refused, for all the aforementioned reasons. I placed a priority on raising our boys to be free-thinkers who stand up against harmful societal norms and advocate for underrepresented minorities by pushing back against patriarchal and discriminatory institutions, and I saw no way I could voluntarily initiate them as members of an organization that I feel is among the worst offenders—especially when they are only babies who have no agency or choice of their own. I understand baptism doesn't mean kids can't ultimately change religions or have no religion at all, but I still viewed it as a commitment to the faith and an affiliation I was uncomfortable making.

We finally agreed that neither of us would "poison the well," so to speak, by being overly preachy or biased when it comes to religion. We've allowed them to go with relatives or friends to Catholic and Protestant church services, and we've waited for them to ask questions and show interest. Right now, my oldest is in sixth grade, and he generally believes in God. He's heard his mom's view, he's heard my view, and while he doesn't know enough to commit to a religion, he's a spiritual kid who simply believes in a higher power. And that's fine. My six-year-old? Staunch atheist. I'm sure part of that is because of me, but he's also a very literal kid who says that Bible stories sound fake and made up. This is an emotionally intelligent and cause-oriented kid whose Christmas present was to ask us to donate ten dollars a month in his name to an organization called Planting Peace, which owns the Equality House across the street from Westboro Baptist Church and is run by my friend Aaron Jackson, because of their work with the gay and trans community, as well as their efforts to deworm children in third world countries.

All of which rebuts a claim I've had leveled at me by many religious folks—that without God and religion, there is no path to goodness, no way to possibly understand right and wrong, good and bad. But I'm raising living proof that you don't need organized religion to have a moral compass. Furthermore, I think being free of the constraints of existing discriminatory beliefs that are deeply entrenched and institutionalized will help parents who are raising children to start with a foundation that isn't riddled with bigotry and intolerance.

I'm not writing this to convert anyone to being a nonbeliever (though that's already happening no matter what I say: a 2015 Pew Research Center poll reported that 34 to 36 percent of millennials (those born after 1980) reported no religious affiliation, adding that this was a dramatic increase from 2007, when only 16 percent of Americans said they were affiliated with no religion[77]). My ask is that parents who are considering raising kids within an organized religion think very carefully about what messages they might be sending if they do so. Children are observant, and they will internalize anything, for example, if your religion tells you to "hate the sin" of same-sex attraction or bars women from serving in positions of power. So, either address it head on and explain why discrimination is wrong and that churches and religions aren't perfect—or you can always hop on over to the heathen bandwagon.

Either way, it never hurts to step back and take an unbiased, holistic view of what you're entering into with your kids. If they hear you preach equality and tolerance outside of church but see you heed a religion that discriminates against women or gay people, that's a potentially harmful mixed message.

77 Michael Lipka, "Millennials Increasingly Are Driving Growth of 'Nones'," *Pew Research Center*, May 12, 2015, https://www.pewresearch.org/fact-tank/2015/05/12/millennials-increasingly-are-driving-growth-of-nones/

Conclusion

Failure Is Not an Option

JUST BEFORE I BEGAN WRITING THIS CHAPTER, I READ ABOUT a thirty-nine-year-old man who body-slammed a thirteen-year-old boy at a county fair because the boy didn't take his hat off during the national anthem. The man fractured the boy's skull.[78] The stats don't lie, and the truth is our boys are getting angrier and angrier, and the instances of violence perpetrated by men are getting more frequent and intense. Misogyny is turned up to eleven on the dial on a daily basis, thanks to examples set by incumbent politicians; sexual assault is rampant in all industries, with multiple men accused of sexual harassment still occupying positions of power; and even Nazis are making a comeback, fueled mostly by angry white men in red hats.

---

78 Chris Boyette, "Montana boy body-slammed for not removing hat during National Anthem, authorities say," *CNN*, August 8, 2019, https:// www.cnn.com/2019/08/08/us/national-anthem-boy-assault-montana/index. html

To say we're at a crucial crossroads for men and society is not an understatement.

But what can you do? You're one person, right? In this maelstrom of toxicity, how can a single person combat these larger social problems that make you feel so hopeless and defeated? Well, if you're the parent of a boy, I say you're in an ideal position of power because you have the opportunity to do the number one most crucial thing on the planet to deal with this crap: you can raise a boy into a man committed to doing and being better.

PARENTING TIP #36: Be a fierce and relentless advocate for boys

I'm so sick of hearing myself have the same conversations over and over again with my boys. I feel like the worst kind of broken record, and the eyerolls and side-eye from my sons when I make them turn off the TV, put their phones and tablets down, and listen to me talk come out in full force. The chances they're ignoring me or tuning me out seem high, and I wonder why I even bother (because aren't kids programmed not to take their parents seriously?).

But then I overhear Will telling his friends that they shouldn't use the word *gay* as an insult. I watch Sam slap on another coat of bright-red nail polish as he shows the world he gives less than zero fucks what anyone thinks of his choices. And Tommy, at age four, will openly rebuke anyone who uses the phrase *like a girl* with negative connotations. Our parental influence will ebb and flow, but you do have the ability to set a foundation for what's good. The stage has been set and the script is written—now your kids just have to read it and act it out in the world. And that only happens when parents commit to raising boys differently.

It. Is. Exhausting. There's no use pretending otherwise. Correcting the misinformation and harmful myths that find their way into our house from school and camp and even from friends and family feels like a full-time job. But these repeated conversations are how change happens. And in addition to instructing your kids, it is also extremely important to model thoughts and behaviors that you want your kids to emulate. It took me a long time to openly admit to my kids that their dad needed to see a professional to seek emotional help because he felt sad. It still makes me anxious and incredibly uncomfortable to say this. But if I don't have honest conversations with my kids in which I'm vulnerable, I can't expect them to reciprocate. I can't risk helping to perpetuate the stereotype of another generation of angry men who don't seek help when they need it because they don't know how to deal with the burden society has laid on them. I can't bear the thought of my kids not being free to be themselves simply because toxic masculinity forbids it.

Would you want to order from one tiny section of a restaurant menu or listen to just one radio station for the rest of your life? Of course not (well, I hope not). But that's how limiting toxic masculinity is for boys. If you don't show them what's available or expose them to different viewpoints and diversity of all kinds, they're much less apt to seek it out and experience it for themselves. Our boys need and deserve to experience the full range of human emotions, not just rage, aggression, violence, and hypermasculinity. They need to know that despite societal opinions to the contrary, they are not limited to bullshit gender roles and rigidly structured ways of thinking. They need to see men cry and talk about their feelings. They need to know men are still men if they paint their fingernails or decide to stay at home with their kids full-time or seek help from a therapist because life circumstances proved too much to bear on their own.

If you as parents don't show them these truths, boys will fall into the lanes society assigns them as males. That's what is at the heart of this issue, and what we have to change. We don't need to vilify the good parts of masculinity, but we do need to differentiate the good from a toxic culture. Strength is an asset, but force is often toxic. Protecting your kids is noble, but overprotectiveness to the point of discrimination and violence is toxic. Providing for your family is essential, but thinking that only applies to money and being a breadwinner? Toxic.

The changes we need to make may seem monumental and too numerous to count, but they're actually a series of small decisions that add up to a societal sea change. And not to sound alarmist, but we're at a crossroads where the decisions we make from here on after will affect the paths we take. Men are killing themselves and each other at a sickening rate, and those who choose not to go down that route are being punished by one another and society for seeking the help they need. It's a self-fulfilling prophecy and a nonsensical downward spiral that we can only stop as parents vowing to raise their kids for a better future. It's not a matter of political correctness, and it shouldn't be a matter of left versus right—it's just the right thing to do for the future generation. Giving boys agency to step out of the insidious box we unfairly put them in is necessary if we're going to change things for the better.

I believe it's possible, and I've seen it work on a small scale. In the spirit of men asking for help when they need it, I'm beseeching every parent of every boy out there to consider small changes that have an outsized impact on society.

Our boys' lives literally depend on it.

ACKNOWLEDGMENTS

IT HAS ALWAYS BEEN MY DREAM TO WRITE A BOOK, BUT DREAMS don't materialize without a lot of help from people who believe in you and who help you along the way.

First, thank you to the Skyhorse team for taking a chance on an unknown person they found on Twitter talking about his son's nail polish. From my first phone call with my editor, Kim Lim, she has been supportive and has helped shape this book from the mess in my head.

Thank you to the MBTA. I wrote this book during my hourlong train rides each way to work, which often turned into ninety minutes thanks to the perpetual train delays, which allowed me to keep writing.

I also need to thank the thousands of people who responded to the initial Twitter thread about Sam's fingernails. From the people who shared it to those who took the time to paint their own nails to send a little kid in Massachusetts messages of support. This wouldn't have been possible without you.

Thank you to my friend Oren Miller, gone too soon, who introduced me to thousands of dads from all backgrounds and walks of life who have taught me an inordinate number of lessons about being a better father and man. Without these fellow brothers in fatherhood, I wouldn't be where I am. Oh yeah, and fuck cancer.

Thank you to all the people who have supported Daddy Files since 2008 when I started this crazy idea. A writer is nothing without an audience, and you've all been so amazing to me. It hasn't gone unnoticed and will never be forgotten.

Falling into some absolutely wonderful feminist and LGBTQIA+ online circles was one of the best things to ever happen to me. Being introduced to people like Lori Day, Nick North, Lisa Hickey, Mark Greene, Amber Leventry, Peggy Orenstein, and Brent Almond has influenced me in ways both large and small, and always meaningful. I'm forever grateful for knowing you all.

Thanks to Alex, who was right all this time and tried like hell to set me straight when I was so, so wrong. I'm sorry I didn't see it sooner, but thanks for sticking with me.

Thank you to my little brother, Nate, who gave me the kick in the butt I needed to start my own website and even paid the initial domain and hosting fees to make it possible. You're a fantastic brother and a spectacular dad yourself. I owe you one.

Acknowledgments

I'd like to acknowledge my parents. My mom, who stayed home with us and made sure she was always involved in our lives. Very involved. Like, driving-the-bus-to-our-away-games-in-high-school-and-directing-the-senior-class-play-while-casting-me-in-the-lead-against-my-will level of involved. And my dad, who worked like a dog to make sure we never went without while simultaneously showing me the power of great writing and storytelling.

Will, Sam, Tommy—I love you all so much, and you continue to teach me lessons I never even knew I needed to learn. You are my life and the reason this book was written. You will be the boys who save us from ourselves.

And finally, MJ. You are my everything and the biggest positive influence in my life. You made sure I had hours of time to write and edit, you propped me up when all I wanted to do was fall apart, and you had confidence in me when I didn't. Nothing good happens without you, and any success I have is because of you. I continue to love you like a madman and am forever grateful you took a chance on me.

© Laura Fiorillo

ABOUT THE AUTHOR

Aaron Gouveia is a former award-winning journalist whose byline has appeared in *TIME, Washington Post, Parents* Magazine, *American Baby,* and the *Huffington Post.* He has also been featured on the TODAY Show, Good Morning America, *People,* Mashable, and *USA Today* to discuss parenting and politics. He started the website The Daddy Files in 2008 to promote involved fatherhood, has contributed to a host of online and print publications on the topic, and is a regular speaker at parenting conferences. His content on topics like gun control and abortion has been seen by millions around the world. When he's not going to Gillette Stadium as a season ticket holder to fanatically cheer on his New England Patriots, he's kayaking and bass fishing in various lakes, ponds, and rivers across New England. Aaron resides in Franklin, Massachusetts, with his wife and three sons.